Broadcast Technology Update

Production and Transmission

Peter B. Seel

August E. Grant

Editors

Focal Press

Boston   Oxford   Johannesburg   Melbourne   New Delhi   Singapore

Broadcast Technology Update

Production and Transmission

Focal Press is an imprint of Butterworth–Heinemann.

Library of Congress Cataloging-in-Publication Data
Seel, Peter Benjamin.
    Broadcast technology update : production and transmission / by Peter B. Seel and August E.
Grant.
        p.   cm.
    Includes index.
    ISBN 0-240-80284-5 (pbk. : alk. paper)
    1. Television—Transmitters and transmission.   2. Audio visual equipment.   3. Digital video.
4. Television broadcasting.   I. Grant, August E., 1956–   . II. Title.
TK6630.S44   1997
621.388'31—dc21   97-4297
                                                                                CIP

British Library Cataloguing-in-Publication Data
A catalogue record for this book is available from the British Library.

Editors   Peter B. Seel
                              August E. Grant
Production Manager   Debra R. Robison
Art Director   Helen Mary V. Marek

The publisher offers special discounts on bulk orders of this book.
For information, please contact:
Manager of Special Sales
Butterworth–Heinemann
313 Washington Street
Newton, MA 02158–1626
Tel: 617-928-2500
Fax: 617-928-2620

For information on all Focal Press publications available, contact our World Wide Web home page at:
http://www.bh.com/fp

10 9 8 7 6 5 4 3 2 1

Printed in the United States of America

Table of Contents

Table of Contents

Preface

This book has two main purposes: (1) to be a supplement to existing production texts that cannot be updated every year, and (2) to be a quick reference for broadcast and telecommunications professionals who need an overview of the latest in audio and video technologies. The rate of change in broadcasting technology is breathtaking and has been accelerated by recent FCC decisions to auction spectrum for digital audio radio broadcasting, and by plans to mandate a U.S. conversion to digital television broadcasting over the next decade.

Schools and universities in North America and other areas of the world are moving to adapt their curricula to this analog-to-digital transition by adding new course content and by adopting new computer-based hardware such as digital audio workstations and non-linear editing systems. The professional broadcast environment is changing even more rapidly as stations and production houses rapidly replace analog gear with digital equivalents that simultaneously increase productivity while adding to production functionality.

The difficulty for broadcasting faculty and professionals alike is finding a printed up-to-date resource that provides basic information about the diffusion of these new technologies throughout the broadcast environment. Broadcasting textbooks published as recently as 1996 are already out of date with regard to contemporary developments in production and transmission technologies. The FCC's December 24, 1996 decision to drop mandated scanning and aspect ratio requirements for the proposed U.S. digital television standard is an example of a significant late-breaking development that will not appear in most contemporary broadcasting texts.

The editors of this book took advantage of digital communications to rapidly assemble the work of experts in every area of audio, video, and lighting technology. The chapters were written in late 1996 and early 1997, then submitted electronically to the editors. The editors revised and passed the chapters back and forth as e-mail file attachments. After editing, chapters and illustrations were sent to Technology Futures, Inc. in Austin, Texas where production manager Deb Robison assembled the book electronically. Finally, the completed book was submitted to Focal Press in camera-ready form. The total elapsed time from the signing of the book contract to publication—four months.

The key point for the reader is that the content of this book is as current as possible considering the state of publishing technology. However, try as we may to keep the content fresh, we recognize that some material is already outdated, given the rate of change in radio and television technologies. To deal with this informational "perishability," Focal Press has created a special Internet Web site for the book—http://www.bh.com/focalpress/02845—that will enable us to provide updates to readers on an ongoing basis. Chapter authors will be working with the editors to provide *viable* links to Web sites that are related to each chapter and to add new content as broadcast technology changes. We expect that most of the content in this book will be valid for a period of two years and that the Web site will be able to provide readers with updates in areas of change. We ask our readers to provide feedback about chapter and Web site content by sending e-mail to the site or to either of us. The volume of change in broadcasting is too great for any one person to assimilate, but with hundreds of readers providing feedback, we anticipate that we can keep the Web site up to date. If you have ideas about additional content or chapters that should be added to the second edition of this book in 1999, please let us know via e-mail or telephone.

We would like to thank all of the authors who contributed chapters to this book. They were selected because of their expertise in discrete areas of audio, video, and lighting technology, and they did a superb job of drafting their chapters and locating illustrations on very short notice. We are grateful that they joined us in this publishing effort and look forward to their contributions to the book's Web site. Our appreciation is also extended to Deb Robison of Technology Futures in Austin, Texas for the hours she spent laying out the book in electronic form for publication. She was the key person in the production process, and we could not have met our publication deadline without her talent and hard work.

We would like to thank Marie Lee, senior editor at Focal Press, for her support of this book. She was an advocate for the book throughout the approval process and has shepherded all of the writing and production efforts. Editorial assistant Karen Sadowski also deserves mention for her skilled handling of many of the crucial day-to-day issues involved in book publication. We appreciate the support of the publication committee and staff at Focal Press for their collective efforts on behalf of this book. We are grateful, as well, for institutional support from our departments: Pete is affiliated with the Department of Journalism and Technical Communication at Colorado State University and Augie was a visitor in the Department of Telecommunications at the University of Georgia during the editing and production process.

Last, but certainly not least, we would like to acknowledge the support and encouragement of our families—Chris, Bobby, and Pookie Grant, and Nanci and P.J. Seel—and for their compassion for those of us who would agree to take on the editing of a book with a four-month production deadline. Their understanding through many late nights, late dinners, and busy weekends is gratefully appreciated.

We hope that the content of the book and the Web site will prove useful to you in your day-to-day worklife and broadcasting studies. In this field, lifelong learning with regard to technology is not optional—it is essential for professional survival. This book is designed to make the process more accessible and a bit easier.

Pete Seel
pseel@vines.colostate.edu

Augie Grant
augie@mail.utexas.edu

February 1997

Broadcast Technology Update

Production and Transmission

1

Introduction

August E. Grant

The most dynamic area of the broadcast industry is not the programming, the stars, corporate maneuvering, or the ratings battles, but the technology used to make all of these other exciting challenges possible. The three-camera method of shooting situation comedies has changed very little in 40 years, but the equipment used to record, edit, and distribute sitcoms has undergone multiple generations of evolution. In many cases where dramatic change has taken place, such as television news, the introduction of new technology has been the enabling force behind these changes.

As a result, one of the biggest challenges faced by broadcasters at any level is keeping up with the latest technologies. This text is designed to help you meet that challenge by exploring and explaining the "state of the art" in most areas of broadcast technology. In doing so, we hope to enable you to take better advantage of the capabilities of new technologies, know the limitations, and be able to compare competing technologies when you must make a decision about whether or when to acquire them. For those of you studying the production process who don't yet have access to the latest technology, we will explain the differences in functionality from one generation of technology to the next so that you will be better prepared for a career in 21st century broadcasting.

It may be argued that the pace of technological change currently being propelled by the conversion from analog to digital technology represents the most radical change in the history of broadcast media, but it is certainly not the first such change. The most similar innovation was the introduction of transistors and other solid-state technology to replace vacuum tubes. The introduction of audiotape (allowing easy recording and editing), videotape (allowing pre-recorded television programming), video editing, color technology, and stereo all represent, to a greater or lesser degree, fundamental changes in the industry.

Process Versus Product Changes

In analyzing the changes resulting from the introduction of these new technologies, it is useful to divide them into two groups: process and product. *Process* changes are those affecting the manner in which programs are produced which have a limited effect upon the look or sound of the final product. Examples of process changes include introduction of new tape formats, cooler lighting systems, wireless microphones and communications gear, digital commercial systems, and automated switching and mixing technology. Audience members are typically not aware of process changes, but they may have a dramatic effect upon the production process.

By contrast, *product* changes are those which have the potential of changing the final product. Color television and stereo (for both radio and television) are the most obvious examples of product changes, both of which were readily apparent to users who had the receiving technology necessary to enjoy the enhancement, but other product changes have become equally important in the production process. The introduction of video effects, from matte keys to DVEs, has changed the look of virtually every television broadcast. Audio and videotape technology has all but eliminated live commercials, and allowed multiple airing of the same programming on both radio and television, while increasing the complexity of the production process.

The line between process and product changes is not well defined. Some changes, such as the use of audio processing equipment or shuttered CCD cameras, will be noticed by some audience members, but not by all. Generally speaking, almost all product changes also require some changes in process, further blurring the distinction between the two. Another complication is that some changes initially designed as process changes may be discovered to have capabilities to enhance the final product that were not part of the original design.

However subtle, the distinction between process and product changes is an important one to consider when studying the innovations that are taking place today within broadcast production facilities. In deciding whether and when to acquire a specific innovation, an important part of the decision process is distinguishing between the process changes that will enhance the efficiency or control over the production process and those which allow a type of audio or visual content that has the potential to distinguish your programming from that of your competitors.

Because most innovations in broadcast production technology are process innovations, most of the innovations discussed in this text are process-oriented. The fact that most of these are based upon the replacement of analog with digital technology, however, suggests the potential for further product innovations as we begin to utilize the capabilities and versatility of digital technology.

Organization of the *Broadcast Technology Update*

The following chapter explores the foundation for the dominant revolution in production technology—the transition from analog to digital technology. Although a few areas of production have been minimally affected by this revolution (for example, lighting), the overwhelming majority of equipment used in 1990 will be replaced by equipment that, for the most part, will not look or work the same as its predecessor.

The remainder of the book is divided into three sections focusing on audio, video, and transmission technologies. Chapter 3, the first audio chapter, explores the range of digital audio recording formats and how they are replacing analog tape in the production process. Chapter 4 then focuses on digital audio workstations and the revolution they have created in the recording and editing process. Chapter 5, the final audio chapter, provides an overview of the latest developments in microphones, mixers, and audio processors, areas in which digital technology slowly continues to improve.

The video section begins with Chapter 6, which explores the latest developments in the most fundamental video production tool—the camera and its lens. The next two chapters explore innovations in the recording process: Chapter 7 focuses on the latest developments in both analog and digital videotape technology, and Chapter 8 reports on video server technology which is providing an interesting option for non-tape-based video recording and playback. The following set of chapters explore the editing process, with Chapter 9 exploring the latest developments in traditional linear video editing, and Chapter 10 introducing innovations in non-linear video editing. New ways of mixing and altering video signals are then discussed in Chapter 11, which explores switchers, special effects, and DVEs. Innovations in lighting technology, particularly in the area of field production, are discussed in Chapter 12.

The fourth section of the book contains two chapters exploring the final link between the broadcast facility and the audience member—transmission technology. Chapters 13 and 14 explore the imminent introduction of digital transmission technology on radio and television, respectively, and the corresponding challenge audience members face in acquiring the necessary reception technologies in order to enjoy digital broadcasts.

The final chapter of the book reflects on implications of the host of developments in broadcast technology discussed throughout this book, including special attention to the adoption of advanced technology in broadcast education.

The authors of individual chapters were selected for their specific expertise in an area of broadcast production, and they were asked to follow a similar format in reporting developments to make it easier for you to move from chapter to chapter. Each chapter provides a brief discussion of the roots and evolution of the components discussed in the chapter, followed by a detailed discussion of the most important recent developments and the current status of each. Finally, each chapter offers a set of "Factors to Watch" to help in predicting and evaluating continuing changes.

Technological change is propelling the broadcast industry into a new era of production innovation. The remainder of this text will provide you a "map" with detailed information about the specific technologies used in the television, radio, and multimedia production processes. It will help you navigate the increasingly interactive, broadband, multichannel broadcast environment.

2

The Transition from Analog to Digital Broadcasting

Peter B. Seel

Global television and radio broadcasting is in the midst of a 30-year metamorphosis from analog to digital technology that will affect almost every area of media technology. Some would say that this process is evolutionary in the sense that the shift is incremental and gradual, but we will argue that, while the transformation may take three decades to complete, it represents a *revolutionary* change in broadcast production and potential modes of transmission. For radio, the advent of digital audio broadcasting (DAB) from satellites or terrestrial towers means improved signal quality, while some radio stations are utilizing applications such as

RealAudio to digitally simulcast their programming over the Internet (Sedman, 1996).

The conversion to digital transmission represents the first fundamental change in television broadcasting since color was added to the NTSC standard more than 40 years ago. It is a transition with multibillion dollar consequences for broadcasters who are the first adopters of these technologies, and consumers who will eventually need to replace their analog radio/TV receivers, VCRs, camcorders, and other related peripherals. It has been estimated that it may cost U.S. television stations $1.2 million to $2.2 million just to pass-through a digital HDTV network signal to their viewers—let alone add their own programming (Weiss & Stow, 1993). Given these astronomical conversion costs, what rationale is there to support such a radical shift in broadcast technology?

Digital Production Issues

The most obvious factor is an improvement in recorded sound and image quality. Digital technology represents an improved method of capturing sound and images as pure data—processing ones and zeroes in a torrent of data transmitted over-the-air and through cables of many types. Media producers have struggled with the distortions inherent in analog technology ever since Edison first recorded sound on tinfoil cylinders in 1877 (Conot, 1987). The sounds engraved into a metal surface were reproduced by a stylus vibrating along the walls of the groove. Today, it seems a crude way of reproducing sound, but it must be remembered that this "primitive" technology provided the technological foundation for "high-fidelity" vinyl records until compact discs replaced them in the 1980s. Digital purity is not everything—some audiophiles still prefer their vinyl recordings to the sonic cleanliness of CDs. The debate over the relative merits of analog versus digital representations of sound and images will continue as digital technology completes its relentless diffusion throughout the world's broadcast institutions early in the next century.

Once images and sounds are captured in digital form, or digitized from analog tape and then transferred to a computer's hard drive, they can be edited in a random-access, non-linear fashion. One of the most tedious aspects of linear tape editing is the time-consuming process of shuttling back and forth to find the desired scene. A non-linear editing system can display an entire screen of small "thumbnail" images of each scene digitized. Editing is accomplished by dragging and dropping each clip into a linear chart of the show to be edited; the clips are then sorted and trimmed to fit. Scenes can be rearranged at will, and digital video effects such as dissolves and special wipes can be inserted as needed between scenes. Non-linear digital editing systems have transformed both video and audio production in the past five years (see Chapters 4 and 10).

Once a news package or broadcast program is edited in digital form, it can be converted back to analog form in a process called "printing to tape." The analog tape is then placed in a cart machine for on-air playback. Increasingly, however, broadcasters skip this process and transfer the program in digital form from an editing computer to another computer server that can play back the segment directly to air. The primary advantage of using digital server technology is that it provides non-linear random access to all the news packages, programs, and commercials stored on it. Rather than loading stacks of videocassettes in a cart machine, the station or network master control operator can randomly air any segment or commercial in any order desired. A newscast rundown can be easily rearranged while the show is on the air. Some large-market television and radio affiliates have already started the conversion to digital server technology, and the process will accelerate as system prices decline and reliability increases (see Chapter 8).

One of the biggest challenges of converting from analog to digital technology is the transition process itself. Digital production technology has been introduced piecemeal in the production process, resulting in systems using different generations of analog and digital equipment side-by-side to produce a final product. One of the last components of the production system to be converted will be the coaxial video cable and shielded audio cable that will eventually be replaced by digital data networks using fiber optics or other high-capacity media.

Digital Transmission

Digital technology also makes it possible to compress broadcast signals so that multiple television signals can be transmitted in a given 6 MHz channel allocation. The Advanced Television Systems Committee (ATSC) digital television (DTV) standard adopted on December 24, 1996 by the Federal Communications Commission (FCC) for the United States would permit broadcasters to transmit one high-definition (HDTV) signal or up to five standard-definition (SDTV) digital signals in the same 6 MHz allotment (ACATS, 1995; Brinkley, 1996b). American broadcasters may become multichannel providers in the daytime hours—mixing traditional soap operas and talk shows with additional all-news, sports, and business channel offerings—while transmitting single-channel, wide-screen HDTV programs and movies in prime time. The digital alchemy of compression makes this possible through mathematical algorithms that enable as much as 95% of the picture information to be discarded prior to transmission—yet still yielding very good picture quality at the receiver.

Futurist George Gilder (1994) argues that the transition to digital broadcasting represents more than incremental improvements in quality and additional programming options. He asserts that the merger of the television and the personal computer—the telecomputer or PCTV—transforms the passive, one-way flow television set into an interactive terminal with full access to the Internet. *Intercasting*, a new term coined to describe the merger of broadcasting and the Internet, would make it possible to view a broadcast program in a window on a personal computer surrounded by supplementary data about the program (Berniker, 1995). The Intercast consortium consists of Intel, NBC, CNN Interactive, Viacom, QVC, America Online, Comcast, Netscape Communications, *Nova* producer WGBH, and PC manufacturers Packard Bell and Gateway 2000. Intel introduced a new "MMX" CPU chip in early 1997 that is designed to enhance multimedia presentation, and it will allow modified PCs to display broadcast television images with supplemental data transmitted in the vertical blanking interval of the TV signal (Fryer, 1996; Paulsen, 1997). NBC plans to transmit news programming with additional information such as digital maps and charts. The digital transmission of radio and television signals will permit the development of new media forms such as intercasting and multichannel program offerings.

The purpose of this chapter is to provide a foundation for the chapters to follow that deal with evolutionary broadcast technologies. It will outline the historical evolution from conventional analog broadcasting to the all-digital systems of the 21st century. A digital broadcasting "primer" will follow to demystify the jargon used to describe new radio, television, and computer-based technologies. A short summary of recent developments will capsulize innovative broadcast technologies that will be covered in greater detail in later chapters. Radio and television transmission issues are specifically addressed in Chapters 13 and 14.

Background—The Evolution of Digital Broadcast Technologies

Figure 2.1 outlines the diffusion of digital technologies in a typical large-market U.S. television station from the mid-1980s to the present day. This trend is then projected into the next millennium. In 1985, the only production-related computers to be found in a television station would have been isolated digital "islands" consisting of non-networked systems for character generation, digital video effects, or weather computer graphics. The one exception was an innovative type of newsroom computer system, such as NewStar, that linked the editorial staff with control room personnel and studio TelePrompTers. The news computer represented the first use of networked digital technology that linked reporters, producers, and directors in a common system that could easily update program content while the newscast was on the air. The digital prompter eliminated the traditional flatbed copy scroller with a system that could modify news content in real time. For any producer who has ever frantically spliced paper news copy onto the flatbed system during a newscast, the digital system represented a significant improvement.

Figure 2.1

The Analog-to-Digital Transition in U.S. Television Broadcasting

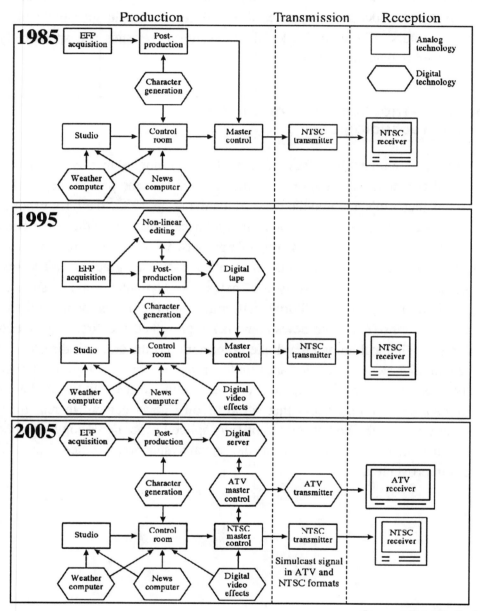

Source: Peter B. Seel

The number of digital islands has increased at present, but the production/transmission/reception broadcast triad still largely consists of analog technology. In radio, digital audiotape (DAT) machines are slowly replacing analog tape, and digital audio workstations (DAWs) are increasingly being used for editing. Many television stations are now using D-2 and D-3 digital tape machines for high-end editing, as well as non-linear editing systems such as Avid, Immix, and Lightworks for program promo production. However, the use of digital editing technology for news at the local station level has been inhibited by the need to digitize field footage from videotape in real time. Thirty minutes of selected footage takes 30 minutes to digitize, a severe limitation for a breaking news story. The recent development of digital field production technologies such as the disk-based Avid/Ikegami CamCutter and the 1/4" Digital Videocassette (DVC) format will eliminate or greatly reduce the time needed to digitize analog field images and sound.

At the network production level, motion picture film is used to record 70% of all prime-time programming (Stow, 1993), but non-linear digital editing systems are now commonly utilized for editing, and digital tape formats are used for time-shifted network program playback across six U.S. time zones. Terrestrial television broadcast transmission and reception are still analog, but direct broadcast satellite (DBS) providers such as DirecTV, USSB, and Echostar are digitally transmitting their multichannel offerings to set-top decoders in subscriber homes. These DBS services had over six million subscribers at the start of 1997—up from 2.2 million at the end of 1995 (McConville, 1996). While the analog-to-digital conversion is well underway at the national production and transmission level, digital technologies are still isolated islands in an analog sea at the local affiliate level. This situation will change radically in the next 10 years.

By the year 2005, analog broadcast systems will be all alone among a host of digital cameras, editing systems, switchers, audio recorders, transmitters, and home receivers. If present FCC plans become law, most U.S. television stations will have until 2012 to convert to the digital ATSC transmission system (FCC, 1992). At that point, the FCC has proposed that analog NTSC television broadcasting will cease, and digital ATV will predominate. A detailed discussion of the implications of this analog-to-digital transition are included in Chapter 14 on television transmission. At some point in the early 21st century, the entire broadcast chain from program acquisition through post-production, transmission, and home reception will be comprised of digital links. The previously-divergent worlds of broadcasting, computer-mediated communication, and telephony will have converged to a point of indistinguishability. This is one of the primary themes of this book, and it will reappear as a thread through all of the chapters.

Digital Media Basics

It may be useful to review some of the commonalties that all digital media share prior to examining each of the respective technologies in the book. First and foremost, once various media are digitized, they can be readily transmitted with high quality through copper wires, fiber optic cables, or through the air. One does not need a broadcast transmitter, per se, to distribute digital signals, only a computer with a digitizing board, some means of compressing the signal, a modem to modulate the signal, and some means of receiving and decompressing the signal at the other end. Nicholas Negroponte (1995) makes the fundamental distinction between sending "atoms" across the country in the form of a mailed CD-ROM, versus sending the same content in the form of digital "bits" over the Internet in real time. Sending data as bits is much faster and cheaper than shipping atoms—as any e-mail devotee can attest.

Negroponte (1995) also notes that communications media such as radio and television that were broadcast over the "air" are now increasingly provided to the home via a cable or wire (the exceptions to this trend are direct broadcast satellite and "wireless cable"—MMDS). Other traditionally wired services such as the telephone are increasingly being provided by wire*less* cellular technologies. This inversion of conventional transmission methods is emblematic of an emerging communications universe based upon wide-bandwidth wired pipelines interconnected with devices that are wireless primarily for mobility.

Digital Replication

Another advantage to non-compressed digital video is that a program can be copied 50 or even 100 times with little degradation in sound or image quality. Since the digital program exists in the form of billions of carefully-ordered zeros and ones, as long as the data is uncorrupted during editing or dubbing, the copy should look exactly like the original. The analog dubbing process introduces noise in the copy, and yields an inherently lower-quality dub with each duplication generation. Anyone who has made a multi-generation copy of a VHS tape is familiar with the results—the image softens and there is smearing in certain colors such as red and yellow. This is not to imply that there is no noise induced in making a digital copy. Bit errors do occur—a zero is misread as a one—but they are controlled by digital error correction or concealment circuits that restore the signal to very close to original quality (Inglis, 1993).

Digital Sampling

Our senses experience the world in analog form—our eyes transform what we see into analog representations of relative brightness, color, and shape. Our eardrums vibrate in direct relation—are analogous—to what we hear. The CCD chip in a video camera captures the image focused upon it in analog form, just as the diaphragm in a microphone mirrors the function of the eardrum. Digital circuitry requires that the analog sound and image be converted to a binary bitstream of zeroes and ones.

Sampling is the conversion process where the analog waveform is transformed into a torrent of perfectly sequenced bits (see Figure 2.2). The analog signal is sampled at a regular time interval and *quantized* by establishing a numerical value that corresponds to the analog signal's amplitude. The numerical value is converted into an 8-, 10-, 16-, 32-, or 64-bit "word" made of a binary code of zeros and ones. The greater the number of samples made per second, the higher the accuracy or quality of the digital image and sound. However, as the number of samples increases, so does the bandwidth required to transmit the digital signal. The conversion process is often abbreviated as A-to-D for analog-to-digital and vice versa. It is important to remember that all digital signals must go through a D-to-A process before we can sense them. Sounds must be reconstituted into waves via a speaker, and images must be displayed as levels of brightness on a screen for our analog eyes and ears to process.

Figure 2.2
Analog-to-Digital Recording

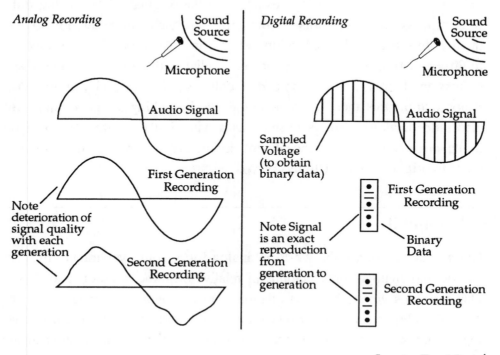

Source: Focal Press[1]

With analog recording methods in audio or video production, noise is introduced as copies are made of the original tape. Generational quality loss was an important consideration for media producers and editors as efforts were made to limit the number of generations from the master. Entire video programs would be re-edited rather than lose a generation in quality. With digital technology, the analog waveform is sampled at regular intervals and quantized into binary zeros and ones that correspond to signal amplitude. Once encoded, the program can be copied repeatedly with very little quality loss. One of the best analogies is that of pouring a beaker full of marbles into another beaker, where the marbles represent program information. With digital recording, all of the marbles are transferred, without any losses, into the second beaker. In analog recording, some marbles are lost in each transfer so that the copies become successively less accurate representations of the original. This explains why the phrase "losing one's marbles" has a special meaning for long-suffering analog audio and video producers.

---

[1] Courtesy of *Radio Production Worktext*, 2nd ed., by Lynne S. Gross & David E. Reese (Newton, MA: Focal Press, 1993), p. 45.

Compression and Decompression

One disadvantage of digital signals is that they require much higher bandwidth to transmit than their analog counterparts. If an analog television signal requires 4.25 MHz for transmission, the bandwidth for its uncompressed digital equivalent would exceed 58 MHz (Inglis, 1993). However, another significant attribute of digital signals is that they lend themselves to being compressed. Much as it easier and less costly to ship 10 ounces of frozen orange juice concentrate than a half gallon of the actual juice, it requires much less bandwidth to transmit a compressed digital program. Just as juice concentrate is created by removing water which is then replaced at the reception end, compression works by discarding redundant data at compression—the excised data is then recreated at decompression. A device called a *codec* (for *co*mpression/*dec*ompression) performs this commonplace digital reconstitution.

The greater the compression ratio, the greater the likelihood that there will be audible or visible artifacts (errors) in the reconstituted version. For this reason, compression can be described as *lossless* or *lossy*. So-called "lossless" compression is achieved at a such a low ratio that there is no audible or visible degradation in the decompressed program. Lossy compression, however, achieves its dramatic reduction in bandwidth at an observable price in quality. Visible artifacts such as pixelation or image blockiness result from too much of the original data being discarded (or poorly reassembled); audio artifacts are heard in the form of sonic dropouts or low fidelity to the original sounds.

JPEG and MPEG Compression

There are two common standards for high-end digital video compression: Motion-JPEG (Joint Photographic Experts Group) and MPEG-1 and -2 (Moving Picture Experts Group). Motion-JPEG is commonly used in non-linear editing systems such as the Avid Media Composer, while MPEG-2 is a toolkit of standards that forms the basis for the proposed ATSC digital transmission system in the United States. The fundamental difference between JPEG and MPEG is that JPEG treats video as series of discrete frames (or still images), while MPEG uses motion interpolation to estimate the changes between frames.

Digital compression is now a commonly-used technology in camcorders such as Digital Betacam, non-linear video editing systems, 150-channel cable systems, direct broadcast satellite systems such as DirecTV and USSB, and the proposed digital ATV transmission system for the United States.

Factors to Watch

The United States is presently in the midst of the transition from analog to digital technology in radio and television broadcasting. As this book goes to press in early 1997, the FCC is writing service rules for satellite-transmitted Digital Audio Radio Service (DARS), a form of digital audio broadcasting. The FCC also plans to hold an auction for DARS spectrum in April 1997 (McConnell, 1997). The advent of DARS broadcasting has been actively opposed by terrestrial broadcasters as a threat to localism which is the foundation of American radio broadcasting. (See Chapter 13 for additional details on this technology and the implications for radio broadcasting in the United States.)

The FCC adopted a digital television standard for terrestrial transmission in December 1996, and the big three networks are making plans for simulcasting DTV programming beginning in the fall of 1998. The first wide-screen DTV sets are expected to go on sale in early 1998 at a premium cost of $1,000 to $1,500 over present set prices (Brinkley, 1996b). The computer industry is planning to manufacture PCs that can also function as DTV receivers. Intel's introduction of the multimedia Pentium MMX chip to enhance PC audio and video presentation is one of the first steps in this process. As the dividing line between televisions and computers blurs and starts to disappear, a battle is shaping up over viewership of digitally-produced programming. In a 1996 speech at the COMDEX trade show, Intel CEO Andrew Grove urged the computer industry to "look outside [its] own backyard for new users" and compete with the television industry "in a war for eyeballs" (Brinkley, 1996a, p. C11). Thus, the analog-to-digital transition for radio and television broadcasters means not only the advent of new and more efficient production/transmission technologies, it also indicates new competition for advertising dollars based upon attendant "eyeballs" or viewership.

In terms of television production, the diffusion of digital video technology (Chapter 7) is a significant development in reducing the cost of digital camcorders and may eventually supplant Super-VHS, Hi-8, and even Betacam formats for electronic field production. DVC is a system adopted by 50 manufacturers, including Sony and Panasonic, that uses 1/4" tape to record one hour of video on a cassette about the size of those used for DAT recording. DVC camcorders manufactured for consumer, prosumer, and professional markets have the potential to bring very high-quality digital video to a wide variety of production environments for under $4,000.

Sony's DVC camcorders are equipped with a unique digital connector known as FireWire (IEEE 1394 standard) that can be used to download digital video directly onto the hard drive of a personal computer, eliminating the need for a video capture card (Waring, 1996). With a powerful PC, software such as Adobe Premiere, and digital source video, high-quality desktop editing will be within the reach of all media producers.

As far as transmission is concerned, the term "broadcasting" will need to be reassessed as alternative modes of program delivery—both wired and wireless—are perfected in the coming decade.

- Telephone companies will be providing cable television service via fiber optic lines.

- Cable operators will be offering data connections to the Internet via coaxial modems.

- Local television affiliates may have evolved into multichannel providers via their DTV spectrum.

These are just a few of the scenarios for terrestrial "broadcasting," without considering what will evolve with DBS providers operating in space. The advent of broadband access to the Internet may also require a reassessment of the term "narrowcasting," as anyone with a computer server and a digital camcorder begins to deliver specialized programming to niche audiences. In an era when ownership of traditional media is increasingly concentrated in fewer and fewer hands, a positive factor is the countervailing trend in technology that will permit greater access for those who know how to create effective media messages.

When digital media technologies first appeared, they were very expensive and appeared to be far beyond the reach of the small market television station or the independent video producer. This is no longer the case. The convergence of television and digital technology in the form of the desktop editing system/character generator/video effects box/audio workstation/3-D animation system means that the fundamental tools of motion media creation are available to all producers, whether they live in Columbus or Copenhagen. On the receiving end, audiences will be able to toggle back-and-forth between conventional broadcast radio and television programming and alternative material available in real time over the Internet. It will be a disconcerting time for broadcasters, but an era that provides a wealth of alternative digital programming for audiences.

Bibliography

Advisory Committee on Advanced Television Service. (1995). *Final report and recommendation*. Washington, DC: Author.

Berniker, M. (1995, October 23). Intel garnering support for "Intercasting." *Broadcasting & Cable*, 74.

Brinkley, J. (1996a, December 12). Defining TVs and computers for a future of high-definition. *New York Times*, C1, C11.

Brinkley, J. (1996b, December 25). FCC clears new standard for digital TV. *New York Times*, C1, C15.

Conot, R. (1987). *Thomas A. Edison*. New York: Knopf.

Federal Communications Commission. (1992). Advanced television systems and their impact upon the existing television broadcast service. *Second report and order/Further notice of proposed rulemaking*, 7 FCC Rcd. 3340.

Fryer, B. (1996, Fall/Winter). PC paralysis. *Newsweek Special Issue*, 48-51.

Gilder, G. (1994). *Life after television*. New York: Norton.

Inglis, A. F. (1993). *Video engineering*. New York: McGraw-Hill.

McConnell, C. (1997, January 6). The many faces of Reed Hundt. *Broadcasting & Cable*, 18-20.

McConville, J. (1996, December 30). Dish prices fall again. *Broadcasting & Cable*, 30.

Negroponte, N. (1995). *Being digital*. New York: Knopf.

Paulsen, K. (1997, January 9). Net, multimedia focus of COMDEX. *TV Technology*, 28.

Sedman, D. (1996). Radio broadcasting. In A. E. Grant (Ed.). *Communication technology update* (5th ed.). Boston: Focal Press.

Stow, R. (1993). Market penetration of HDTV. In S. M. Weiss & R. L. Stow (Eds.). *NAB 1993 guide to HDTV implementation costs* (Appendix II). Washington, DC: National Association of Broadcasters.

Waring, B. (1996, January 2). Digital video's new age. *New Media*, 17.

Weiss, S. M., & Stow, R. L. (1993). *NAB 1993 guide to HDTV implementation costs* (Appendix II). Washington, DC: National Association of Broadcasters.

II

Audio Production Technologies

Until quite recently, the most prevalent medium in the professional audio production world was 1/4-inch analog reel-to-reel tape. A talented audio engineer was judged by how many edits she or he could make in an hour with a single-edged razor blade and splicing tape. Trimmed sections were dumped in a pile with the fervent prayer that the editor would not have to dig through the stack to find a segment removed in error. A long audio project or a non-professional narrator could generate a very large pile of trimmed tape. There were other more mundane hazards—a magnetically-charged razor blade could leave audible pops at each edit point if the editor was not careful.

Those were the "good ol' days" in audio production prior to the diffusion of digital audio recording and editing systems. These new technologies have transformed audio production in the past decade. While razor blades can still be found in many production facilities, it is far more routine to encounter digital audio workstations that can make very precise edits while keeping all the trims at hand if needed. As these technologies have diffused through the professional audio production world, schools and colleges have also moved from razor-blade editing to digital production systems. Computer-literate students often feel right at home editing with a mouse and a graphical representation of the soundtrack on a screen. They recognize that this is going to be the technology they will use in their future professional careers.

The purpose of this section is to review the latest developments in audio production technologies for broadcasting. Chapter 3 is a survey of digital audio playback and recording technologies that range from DAT to DVD. Since the number of digital formats continues to increase, this chapter is a valuable resource in comprehending the production advantages and disadvantages of each format. The irony is that, while these new tools have greatly increased audio production processing and editing capabilities, they have added a level of complexity not found with analog tape. An audio "scorecard" is now needed to keep track of all the digital formats available.

Chapter 4 is a review of the present state of development in digital audio workstations (DAWs). These processing and editing systems are emblematic of the analog-to-digital transition in audio production technology for broadcast. These non-linear, "non-destructive" systems allow the engineer or editor to visualize the soundtrack on screen as they work. All the trimmed material is saved in memory and ready to be reinserted with an undo command, rather than searching through the trim pile in the analog tape days. DAW systems also add many of the audio processing capabilities formerly found in a full rack of very expensive noise reduction and effects boxes in the analog studio. Moore's Law states that the capabilities of digital systems will double every 18 months, indicating the likelihood that the power of DAWs systems will continue to increase while prices will remain constant or decrease. This is good news for all audio producers—student or professional.

Chapter 5 focuses on the audio mixers, processors, and microphones used in contemporary radio and audio production facilities. As experienced audio engineers are aware, the strength of the audio "chain" from the mouth of the broadcaster to the ear of the listener is based on the weakest link. This chapter reviews all of the key elements in the chain and the technologies that enhance the delivery of the highest-quality signal to the listener or viewer. The author provides detailed information and comparative costs to enable the reader to make decisions about the value of the systems discussed.

The audio production environment for broadcasting has changed more in the past 10 years than in the entire half-century since the development of magnetic recording during World War II. The shift to digital technology has influenced every aspect of audio production, and it is anticipated that new developments in this area will require that audio professionals constantly retrain themselves to stay current in the field. Perhaps the day will soon come when we can finally toss out that old box of unused razor blades.

3

Broadcast Digital Audio Formats

D. William Moss

One area in which the impact of digital audio has been deeply felt is broadcasting. The capabilities and advantages of digital audio storage and production formats are tailor-made for the intermediate-level production tasks, high storage requirements, and accessibility demanded by broadcast operations. Radio, in particular, has embraced digital audio wholeheartedly, not just in the form of the familiar compact disc, but also as a production, logging, and archiving format. Television commonly makes use of hard-disk-based digital audio workstations for post production tasks. There are a variety of digital audio media and formats commonly used in broadcasting today.

Most digital audio applications in broadcasting are based around "small format" technologies. These are systems designed for flexible, sophisticated production and archiving of audio material with fewer than 16 tracks, generally in compact media. Often, these formats are stereo only. Large format digital audio technologies remain the province of professional music production and film and prime-time television post-production. Digital audio formats for broadcast also overlap much more with consumer formats than most other professional digital video and audio formats.

The Transition to Digital Audio

The defining force in the evolution of broadcast audio formats since the early 1980s has been the transition from analog formats to digital ones. In the early 1980s, the principal tools of broadcast audio were long-playing records, NAB audio cartridges, analog reel-to-reel tape (which is still in widespread use), and medium-format analog multi-track systems. The advent of the compact disc in 1983 forever changed radio, as durable, small CDs became the favored archiving media. Shortly thereafter, digital audio-tape (DAT) was commercially released, and it began displacing expensive, inconvenient reel-to-reel tape formats.

By far, the most fascinating development in digital broadcast audio has been the emergence of non-linear formats based on computer hard disk and magneto-optical disk media. Computers play a prominent role in modern broadcast audio, and non-linear digital audio workstations are widely used in both radio production and video and television post-production. In many broadcast facilities, analog audio formats are now an afterthought, used only for the archiving of legacy material.

The Current Generation of Digital Audio Formats

There are several digital audio formats in widespread use in broadcasting. In general, there are two distinct uses for digital media and formats: production and archiving. *Production* formats allow multiple rewriting of audio information and often have the capability for multiple tracks of simultaneous audio. Currently, hard-disk-based non-linear formats are becoming popular for production. *Archiving* formats allow easy access to program material; high storage capacity in a small, inexpensive package; and, ideally, durability. The compact disc is currently the most popular archiving and programming format, although DAT is also widely used and hard-disk systems are making inroads as well.

Table 3.1
Summary of Common Digital Audio Media
for Broadcasting

Format	Read/Write	Capacity at CD Quality	Applications
Compact Disc	Read-only or WORM	74 minutes	Program material, archiving
Minidisc	Write many	74 minutes	Incidental program material
DAT	Write many	120 minutes	Logging, archiving, program material, EFP
Digital Multi-track Tape	Write many	Varies	Production
Magneto-optical	Write many	Varies. approx. 90 min./GB	Production
Hard Disk	Write many	Varies: approx. 90 min./GB	Production, incidental program material

Source: D. William Moss

The Compact Disc

The compact disc is familiar to consumers as the common format for consumer audio products. Co-developed primarily by Sony and Philips, audio CDs first came to the consumer market in 1983, and rapidly found widespread acceptance (Pohlman, 1995). Since the success of the audio compact disc, the CD medium has been adapted into various data formats including the common CD-ROM format.

The audio CD format uses a physical standard called Red Book that differentiates it from CD-ROM (Yellow Book) and other related formats (McFadden, 1996). Essentially, audio compact discs can hold up to 74 minutes of uncompressed, stereo digital audio information using a 44.1 kHz sampling rate with 16 bit resolution. That sampling rate and resolution defines "CD-quality sound," although it represents a compromise between sound quality and storage requirements. The attraction of broadcasters to CD is because of several factors. Compared with media such as vinyl records, reel-to-reel tape, cassette tape, and digital audiotape, compact discs offer a superb combination of high-quality sound, random access, durability, and small size. Consequently, CDs have created a niche for themselves as the standard format for the storage of program material in most commercial radio stations. Compact discs are also commonly used to distribute and archive production material such as sound effects and production music. The compact size and high storage density make it possible to keep an entire library of audio content in a very small space.

The technology to reliably and conveniently record to compact discs (CD-R) has become commonly available in the mid-1990s (Pohlman, 1995). Although this technology is generally used for creating CD-ROMs for computers as opposed to audiodiscs, the ability to cheaply master to durable CDs with the CD-R format is attractive to broadcast organizations looking for an archiving medium more durable and convenient than DAT and other linear storage media. It is also more cost effective than hard disk or magneto-optical (MO) media. One drawback is that the compact disc remains a write-once/read many (WORM) medium, unlike most other formats which allow repeated re-recording.

A medium related to compact disc but not yet in widespread use is the "digital versatile disc," also known as DVD. It is significantly more advanced than CD in terms of storage capacity and features and is discussed later in this chapter.

The Minidisc

The minidisc (MD) format was released by Sony in 1992. Designed to be the successor to analog cassette tapes, the MD offers features common to cassettes and compact discs. Like the compact disc, the minidisc is a random-access format that holds up to 74 minutes of digital audio. Unlike

CDs, the minidisc format uses data compression in a 5:1 ratio to fit 74 minutes of audio into the 140 MB of storage available on a single minidisc, rather than the 680 MB available on a CD (Woudenberg, 1996). Also, unlike CDs, the minidisc is a magneto-optical format that allows repeated recording and erasing of stored audio, similar to an audiotape. The data compression in a minidisc is "lossy"; that is, it causes a subtle but audible degradation in sound quality compared with the original audio signal (Woudenberg, 1996).

The small loss in sound quality has not prevented MD from assuming a role in professional broadcasting. The write-many feature of the minidisc, combined with its very small size and random access capabilities, have made MD one successor to the analog cartridge tape, or "cart," commonly used by radio and television stations for storing incidental program material such as commercials and promotional spots (Pohlmann, 1995). Minidisc-based cart machines are now replacing analog cartridge decks in many radio studios. The quality loss in minidisc is small enough to be unnoticeable after broadcasting. Although it is finding a niche in broadcasting, MD is not having the success as a consumer format that was originally anticipated. It may end up being a transitional format, facing replacement when a write-many uncompressed format based around a similar technology or when high-capacity DVD type formats become common.

Digital Audiotape

Introduced in 1987, the rotary-head digital audiotape format has found widespread acceptance as a broadcast format. Popularly known simply as DAT, this format combines the advantages of digital quality and consistency with the write-many capabilities of typical magnetic media (Pohlmann, 1995). Although developed to be both a consumer and professional format, the high cost of DAT decks has kept the consumer market quite small. DAT decks have become standard features of many broadcast studios, however, where they are used for mastering audio productions and for logging and archiving program material and productions.

DAT tape incorporates all the advantages of digital encoding. The quality of DAT recordings is equal to that of compact discs; it can be even better, with most DAT decks supporting sampling rates of 48 kHz, as well as 32 kHz and 44.1 kHz. DAT does not use compression, so there is none of the signal degradation associated with MD. Professional DAT decks also have digital audio inputs and outputs, allowing for completely digital throughput when mastering productions from digital workstations or copying material from compact disc. Many higher-end models support synchronization protocols, making them ideal for video post-production where it is necessary to chase and lock with videotape decks or digital workstations. DAT cassettes are extremely small, about half the size of a standard analog cassette. Combined with the ability of many professional DAT decks to record longer times at lower fidelity—and the development of high-capacity cassettes using thin tape—the DAT format makes an excellent logging and archiving medium.

Although DAT offers the write-many feature conspicuously absent from CD and CD-R, it suffers from some of the drawbacks of all linear media. Even though DAT offers very fast winding speeds and sophisticated, subcode-based time code and start ID recording, it cannot provide true random access. Both DAT tapes and DAT decks also tend to be fragile, although there are now reliable portable DAT decks for field use. The helical scan technology used in DAT drives is complex, and high-end, feature-laden professional DAT decks can cost considerably more than high-end CD players. DAT has become a popular format for broadcast production, however. Until an uncompressed, random access format offers true write-many capabilities combined with low-cost media, DAT technology should remain widespread.

Digital Multi-Track Tape Formats

Many broadcast operations use multi-track recording systems for sophisticated audio production and video post-production. Although hard disk and magneto-optical disk-based systems are supplanting tape in many broadcast production studios, the convenience and relative cheapness of linear, tape-based digital formats have kept them competitive. Although there are large-format digital tape formats that support 24- and 48-track recording, broadcasters tend to use smaller, less expensive formats that provide a combination of flexibility and cheap media. Two commonly available eight-track formats are the Alesis ADAT and Tascam DA-88.

The Alesis and Tascam systems share many basic similarities. They both offer eight tracks of independent digital audio at either a 44.1 kHz or 48 kHz sampling rate with 16-bit resolution. They are both designed around helical-scan, revolving heads derived from videotape technology (similar to stereo DAT). They both also record onto standard videotape cassettes, the ADAT using S-VHS cassettes, and the DA-88 using Hi-8 cassettes (Pohlmann, 1995).

For radio production and many kinds of video post-production, random access hard-disk based editing can be difficult to beat. But there are some advantages to tape-based formats. The primary advantage is that tape-based systems allow huge amounts of storage very cheaply. The ADAT will record up to 40 minutes of eight-track information at CD quality on one S-VHS cassette, while the DA-88 can pack nearly two hours of eight-track information onto a very compact Hi-8 cassette. In situations where there is a great deal of material that must be permanently archived, or where multiple productions must be hosted on the same system, that economy of storage can be very desirable when compared with the 2.6 GB hard drive or magneto-optical drive that would be necessary to host one hour of eight track, CD-quality data in a digital workstation. These systems also allow multiple units to be synchronized, providing nearly unlimited track space. The lack of random access is a severe disadvantage, however, and digital workstations are becoming the standard as they become less expensive and easier to use. As random access systems continue to penetrate the broadcast market, tape-based formats will remain more entrenched in music production where linear storage is less of a disadvantage.

Hard Disk and Magneto-Optical Formats

The advent of hard-disk-based audio storage and production technology has been one of the most important recent developments in the field of broadcasting. As the costs of powerful computers and high-capacity digital storage media have fallen, digital workstations and hard-disk-based archiving systems have moved out of the realm of the esoteric and into broadcast production facilities around the world. The fact is that, in most situations, hard-disk-based production and archiving systems offer an unbeatable combination of sophisticated production features, ease of use, and flexibility. Digital audio workstations and their features are discussed in more detail in Chapter 4.

Digital audio workstations and digital archiving systems would not be practical if high-capacity hard disk drives had not dropped drastically in price in the last few years. As of early 1997, a 1 GB or 2 GB hard drive configured for audiovisual applications can be purchased for a few hundred dollars. Considering the high storage requirements of multi-track sound, the drop in price from a few thousand dollars in the late 1980s has been a key step in making digital sound editing accessible.

Hard disks offer a combination of features that is uniquely suited to audio production (Pohlmann, 1995). They are a true random access medium, much like CDs and minidiscs, and they can be partially or completely rewritten *ad infinitum*. Unlike either of those formats, however, individual hard disk drives allow storage of up to 9 GB of data, with arrays of multiple drives supporting storage of dozens or even hundreds of gigabytes of data. Hard disk drives also access, read, and write data dozens of times faster than CD or MD drives. That makes them a practical medium for editing and processing sound, as well as storing it for playback.

All of the advantages of hard disks do not come without a literal price, however. Despite the huge drop in prices for hard disk drives, they remain an order of magnitude more expensive per MB of storage than either CD-R discs or minidiscs. They are also fragile and must be treated delicately. Finally, in general, they are not portable, and they require an expensive computer to be of any use.

Some of the disadvantages of hard disk drives as an audio storage medium have been somewhat countered by the development of removable media drives based on magneto-optical disks. Magneto-optical disks use a hybrid of optical technology such as that found in CDs, and magnetic technology as used in traditional hard disk drives. Minidiscs are a magneto-optical technology and demonstrate some of the advantages of this medium. MO disks are in cartridges and can be swapped in the drive, much like CDs or cassette tapes. As a medium, they are more durable than hard disk drives. They are also available in high capacities—up to 2.6 GB. They are not quite as fast as hard disk drives when accessing or reading or writing, but they are a better and cheaper medium for long-term archiving of audio data.

Table 3.2
Basic Feature Comparison of Similarly Tasked
Analog and Digital Formats

	Analog Format	Digital Format
Program Material	*LP Record*: Semi-linear, fragile, degrades with use. 30 minutes storage × 2 sides. Non-recordable.	*Compact Disc*: Nonlinear, durable, does not degrade with use. 74 minutes storage × 1 side. Non-recordable.
Incidental Material	*NAB Cart*: Linear. Degrades with use. Up to 15 minutes storage per unit. Large per-unit size for cartridges.	*Minidisc*: Nonlinear. Minimal degradation with repeated use. 74 minutes storage per unit. Small per-unit size for discs.
Archiving	*Reel-to-Reel Tape*: Degrades with use. Linear. Copies with generational signal loss. No subcode information. Can be edited by hand. Large per-unit size for tapes.	*DAT*: Degrades with use but can be copied with no signal loss. Linear. Includes subcode information (time code, start IDs). Cannot be edited by hand. Small per-unit size for tapes.
Production	*Multi-Track Tape*: Degrades with use. Linear. Individual tracks may not be edited. Large per-unit size for tapes. Easily archived.	*Digital Workstation*: Does not degrade with use. Non-linear. Individual tracks may be edited. Small per-unit size for drives. Expensive to archive.

Source: D. William Moss

One practical application of hard-disk-based audio formats is worth commenting on in detail. In recent years, hard-disk systems have made dramatic inroads into radio stations, largely as production tools. But, they have also proved to be a valuable means of archiving and retrieving supplemental program material, such as commercials, promotional spots, liners, bumpers, and sound effects. A large commercial radio station may have several thousand of these separate audio pieces in various kinds of rotation at any time.

Traditionally, material such as this has been recorded on NAB carts, and hundreds or thousands of carts have had to be kept on file by large stations. Hard-disk systems offer a vast improvement in convenience and space over traditional, cart-based archiving and playback. There are several computer and hard-disk products on the market now that allow a station to archive several hundred minutes of spots and effects on one or two GB of disk space, and to retrieve and playback these pieces using a simple, intuitive interface and cataloguing system. The more sophisticated of these systems, known as digital commercial systems (DCS, see Figure 3.1) will accept scheduling information from the programming log, and automatically cue up the correct spots and even play them. Many of them will also network with digital audio workstations, making possible a nearly tapeless radio station. Systems such as these have played a large role in the automation of modern radio stations.

Figure 3.1
Typical DCS System

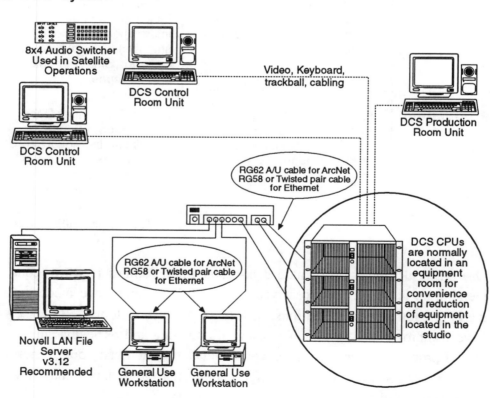

Source: Computer Concepts Corporation

Factors to Watch

Digital audio formats have become the standard in audio production and archiving for broadcast, but the creators of digital audio standards and media are not resting on their laurels. Development of new formats and new technologies continues, with the pace of development and innovation increasing as the computer power and storage needed to make digital formats work become less expensive.

Although it is not developed enough to warrant detailed coverage here, one medium worth watching is the digital versatile disc. DVD was commercially released in the winter of 1996, and is expected to be the successor to the compact disc and the video laserdisc. DVD offers a minimum of approximately seven times the storage space of a compact disc in an equivalently sized, downward-compatible format. Eventually, a single DVD may store up to 17 GB, compared with .68 GB on one CD. That opens the door for much more efficient information storage at CD quality, or storage of equivalent amounts of much higher-quality audio information, as well as high-quality video (Hughes, 1996).

One factor that is already proving important is the increasing integration of digital audio formats and systems within studios and production houses. The compact disc codified the basic digital audio quality standard as 16 bit/ 44.1 kHz, and many pieces of digital audio equipment accommodate this standard. DAT, digital workstations and computer audio formats, and digital effects processors all can operate at this level of quality (and often at higher quality). With networked production systems, audio content can now be produced digitally, stored digitally, recalled from hard disk digitally for play on air or use in video post-production, archived digitally to CD-R or DAT, and transferred digitally between different pieces of equipment and production stages. This continuity of the digital domain allows unprecedented flexibility and audio quality within the production and broadcast chain.

Bibliography

Hughes, K. (1996). *DVD FAQ.* [On-line]. Available: http://www.cd-
info.com/CDIC/Technology/DVD/dvd-faq.html.

McFadden, A. (1996). *CD-R FAQ*. [On-line]. Available: http://www.cd-
info.com/CDIC/Technology/CD-R/FAQ.html.

Pohlmann, K. (1995). *Principles of digital audio*. New York: McGraw Hill.

Woudenberg, E. (1996). *Minidisc frequently asked questions*. [On-line]. Available:
http://www.hip.atr.co.jp/~eaw/minidisc/minidisc_faq.html.

4

Digital Audio Workstations

Nancy L. Reist

The year is 1984. As part of his re-election campaign, President Reagan has just made a major speech. Radio reporters across the United States are scrambling to prepare for the "afternoon drive" newscasts. They dub key statements from the speech onto a reel of tape, mark the segments they want to use, cut the tape with razor blades, and reassemble the pieces. These pieces are then inserted into a production or played sequentially for live analysis and commentary.

Fast-forward to the presidential campaign of 1996, and you will see some significant changes. Reporters still hustle while they sort material from President Clinton's campaign messages, but many of them are working on specially-configured personal computers called digital audio workstations

(DAWs). DAWs enable radio reporters to manipulate audio from Clinton's speech in much the same way that their print counterparts use word processors to organize text. Reporters can easily rearrange, delete, or copy segments of sound. If they don't like the changes they've made, they simply "undo" them.

Fundamentally, DAWs are computers that process sound. They are now widely used in a variety of situations including broadcast news production, video and film post-production, radio production, multimedia production, and music mastering. Many DAWs operate using a Macintosh or PC, while others come with a proprietary computer. Most professional DAWs include sophisticated analog-to-digital (A-to-D) and digital-to-analog (D-to-A) circuitry. However, as the sound capabilities of home computers improve, low-cost, software-only DAWs are becoming more common. Although DAWs come in a wide variety of configurations, they share two important attributes: the non-linear storage of digital information and the visual display of audio information.

Visual Display of Audio

DAWs supplement the information audio engineers get from listening to sounds with pictures that represent the sound waves (see Figure 4.1). The detail of the display varies with the system, but many DAWs permit users to view a picture of the sound at the sample level. They can then set transition points in precise locations, making much tighter edits and more complex mixes than would have been possible with conventional analog techniques. Some DAWs can also provide a visual display of the frequency spectrum of a sound wave, which helps audio engineers eliminate unwanted noise such as hum.

Figure 4.1
Computer Rendering of a Sound Wave

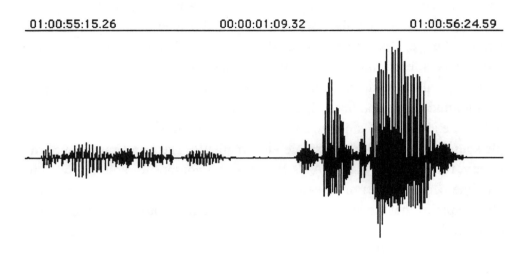

01:00:55:15.26   00:00:01:09.32   01:00:56:24.59

Source: Nancy L. Reist

Non-Linear Storage

In analog production, and in some other digital formats such as DAT, audio information is stored sequentially in a physical space. Audio engineers need to locate and access the particular place where the audio is stored in order to manipulate it. This can be a fairly unwieldy process, particularly when the production is long and includes many different sounds. Conversely, DAWs store audio information on a computer's hard drive in available spaces, regardless of their location. Parts of a file can be in one place, while the rest is stored elsewhere. The computer keeps track of the locations of various audio segments and can access different clusters of sound rapidly and play them together seamlessly. Thus, audio can be played in any order, depending on the instructions the audio engineer gives the DAW. Editing becomes "non-destructive," because commands detailing playback order have replaced the need to physically remove or move unwanted audio. This means that audio engineers can do much more elaborate editing than would otherwise be possible. The "T-Rex smashes the Explorer" scene in *Jurassic Park*, for example, contained thousands of edits (Skywalker Sound, 1996).

Non-linear storage also allows audio engineers to manipulate the way different audio segments are played. In essence, this means that once the sound is recorded, a DAW can be configured as a virtual multi-track mixer. DAWs differ in the number of streams of audio they can play simultaneously. Many can play up to eight, while some can handle 16 or more. On most DAWs, each individual segment can be played at a different volume. Many also allow audio engineers to apply a variety of fades or even to draw an amplitude envelope that adjusts fades in multiple locations (see Figure 4.2). The ability to customize cross-fades is vital when sounds from multiple sources are mixed into a single environment. The San Francisco Symphony, for example, uses DAWs to produce a composite radio show from multiple performances of the same piece. The program's producer, Jack Vad, explains that the variable cross-fade points and adjustable curves of the Sonic Solutions software he uses are very important for making seamless transitions (Reist, 1994a).

Most DAWs also provide the option of automating the final mix. In addition, since the playback sequence is not constrained by the physical location of the audio, individual segments can be used many different times without the need for copying and its associated loss of quality. Many DAWs have built upon this advantage by allowing a wide range of special effects, such as loops, delays, and reverbs.

Background

DAW technology began to affect audio production in the late 1980s, and, initially, its use was limited to complex, high-budget production houses. Producers discovered that, once they had mastered the technology, they could mix and edit more quickly and precisely using DAWs. For example, David Gans, a veteran radio producer, was immediately impressed with the versatility of DAWs when he hosted the live national radio broadcast of the Grateful Dead's 1991-1992 New Year's Eve concert. The production crew used two Digidesign DAWs to produce many pre-recorded segments that were incorporated into the live broadcast, some of which were produced after the concert began. Gans reported that the DAWs allowed him to ask the audio engineer for changes that would have been impractical in the analog world:

If I had been doing that on multi-track, it would have been tear your hair out time. It would have meant re-editing the two-track on that particular cue and laying everything else in again. Here, all he had to do was shorten the cue that we were talking about, and everything else just laid itself back in sequence. The versatility of the tools and the skill of the editors were a real joy from a creative standpoint. It enabled things to be done that a year or two ago would not have been possible (Reist, 1992, p. 11).

Figure 4.2

Amplitude Envelope to Adjust Sound Levels in an Audio Sample

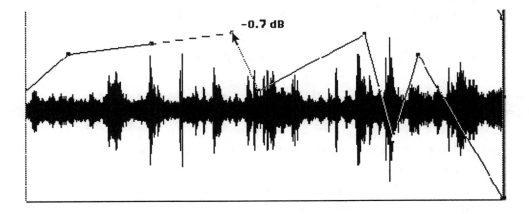

Source: Nancy L. Reist

Although many audio engineers, including Gans and Vad, were quick to acknowledge the advantages of working with DAWs, a number of questions and problems limited the adoption of DAWs in the early 1990s. Cost was, of course, an important constraint. The original workstations themselves were prohibitively expensive for many studios, and the cost of storage added to that. Even if a studio could afford a DAW system, the decision about which system to purchase daunted many. The market was flooded with competing DAWs, many of which used proprietary file formats that limited the exchange of files between systems. In addition, other key features vary from system to system, influencing—and sometimes confusing—the selection process.

Backup

Most computers fail from time to time, and DAWs are no exception. Therefore, a fast, easy, reliable backup system is critical. The backup copy may be stored on a variety of media, such as another hard drive, Exabyte tape drives, optical drives, or DATs. Most systems require the audio engineer to make periodic backup copies of files, which may be very time consuming. A few high-end systems offer automatic backups.

User Interface

While DAWs give audio engineers much more flexibility and control over the sound, they are not necessarily easier to use than traditional analog technologies, and many require fairly advanced computer skills to operate. Some DAW manufacturers have addressed this problem through the design of on-screen graphics and menus to help the user. Other DAWs include optional controllers which mimic the controls of traditional tape recorders and consoles.

Networking

Some DAWs can be configured into networks so that more than one workstation can access the same audio files. When this feature is combined with the potential for limiting access to non-destructive editing, it can be a very powerful tool for large production facilities. Multiple audio engineers can use the same library of sound effects, music, and dialogue simultaneously. So, for example, when President Clinton gives a radio address, National Public Radio can record it into its Sonic Solutions network, enabling individual producers to use appropriate sound bites for their stories.

Synchronization

Many DAWs include SMPTE time code, which is essential for synchronizing audio to video, film, or other audio sources. Some advanced systems also offer machine-control interfaces that allow the DAW to serve as master or slave to video-production devices. A few offer full VTR-emulation capabilities for a direct interface with video editors.

Input/Output

Most professional DAWs provide both digital and analog inputs and outputs, and the number of each varies with the system. This is an area where DAW advertising may be somewhat misleading, since the number of tracks advertised usually refers to the number of streams of audio or "virtual" tracks the system can play simultaneously. A DAW may be described as an "eight track," when, in fact, it only has two inputs and two outputs.

Sampling Rate

Most DAWs can operate at a variety sampling rates, but they can only use a single rate throughout a specific project. The two most common are 44.1 kHz (the sampling rate of audio CDs) and 48 kHz (the sampling rate used by most broadcasters for original material). Sound sampled at a rate that differs from other sounds in a given production will play at an altered speed and pitch. Sample rate converters can convert files to the appropriate sample rate, but they usually have an audible impact on the signal. Converting the signal to analog and then resampling at the appropriate sampling rate also degrades the signal.

Other Features

Other important features included in some DAWs include:

- The ability to redraw the wave to edit out "pops."

- The ability to set different zoom levels for each track.

- Audio scrub capability.

- Double-speed playback.

- Multiple levels of undo/redo.

Recent Developments

DAWs have become commonplace in production facilities that use audio. Undoubtedly, increased affordability is the single most important factor contributing to the rapid increase in DAW penetration during the mid-1990s.

Although high-end dedicated systems are still extremely expensive, a number of versatile, high-quality DAWs are available in the $3,000 to $4,000 range, making them a cost-effective alternative. The drop in price is due, in part, to the availability of cheaper RAM and digital storage. In addition, many basic personal computers now come equipped with sound cards and software that permit playback, recording, and simple manipulation of sound files.

File size remains an important limitation for DAWs, not only for storage, but also for file transfers. This issue has become increasingly important as DAWs rely more heavily on local area networks and even the Internet to exchange files. A minute of stereo, CD-quality audio requires 10 MB of storage space. In order to reduce the file size, many DAWs now incorporate optional or mandatory audio data compression. Compression ratios of 4:1 are common, while some systems have ratios of 10:1 or even higher. Current compression formats, such as those developed by Dolby and MPEG, use perceptual coding, which relies on the human ear's inability to detect certain kinds of signal losses. This coding remains controversial, however. Some audiophiles maintain that the quality of compressed signals is significantly reduced, while others assert that the loss is minimal. More troubling is the signal degradation that can occur when the audio is exposed to repeated applications of perceptual encoding and decoding cycles. While this is unlikely within a DAW, the audio produced by the DAW may encounter perceptual compression during subsequent post-production, broadcast and satellite distribution, station time-shift recording, adaptation for multimedia production, and consumer recording (Pizzi, 1996b). Thus, audio engineers should consider the treatment their productions will encounter after they leave the DAW before applying perceptual encoding.

The increased acceptance of the Open Media Framework (OMF) file format has improved the practicality of DAW systems which support it. The OMF format allows audio engineers to transfer audio files—and in some cases, even editing, mixing, and processing instructions—between different models of DAWs. This means that projects produced on DAWs can be moved more easily between production facilities. Furthermore, owners who wish to replace their DAWs with a different system will be able to access archived files—as long as both systems support OMF.

Another factor that has contributed to the increasing penetration of DAWs is the recent proliferation of specialized systems. The needs of film studios, independent radio producers, CD-ROM producers, and DVD producers are vastly different. By designing systems that include only the tools needed by specific kinds of users, manufacturers are able to reduce the cost and simplify the user interface. In April 1996, for example, Sonic Solutions introduced SonicStudio, a family of DAWs, each customized for specific applications. SonicStudio Master, designed for high-end audio mastering, includes features such as sample-accurate editing, high-resolution filtering, and advanced control of CD subcode data. SonicStudio OnAir, on the other hand, was developed in conjunction with National Public Radio and is designed to provide radio producers with real-time audio production tools, including:

- Multiple simultaneous records and playback for the capture of network feeds and reports from the field.

- Double-speed playback to facilitate editing.

- Multiple set-ups, which can be stored to allow producers to quickly set up the computer in the configuration that is appropriate for the task at hand (Sonic in the News, 1996).

The sophistication and variety of the signal processing that accompanies DAWs has also improved. The most common and important processors for most applications include equalization and amplitude processing, although time compression, pitch shift, delays, and reverbs are also very popular. Some systems provide real-time signal processing which allows adjustments during playback, but many DAWs must record processed sounds into new disk files before they can be played. While many DAWs include a variety of processors as part of the basic package, others have embraced the plug-in concept, which allows operators to purchase the specific processing tools they need as add ons. In addition to the basic processing that accompanies the DAW, Digidesign's ProTools, for example, accommodates a wide variety of third-party processing plug-ins (Trubitt, 1996).

Factors to Watch

While the price of memory, storage, and computers may stabilize or even rise slightly in the next couple of years, DAWs already are cost effective. The penetration of DAWs should continue to grow, and they should gradually replace their analog counterparts in most production facilities. Recent trends in improved interface design, increased processing and compression capabilities, wider implementation of the OMF file format, and the development of specialized systems should continue.

Important ethical and legal issues accompany the growing popularity of DAWs. The questions associated with assigning and protecting copyrights that were introduced with digital samplers become even more complicated with DAWs, since audio can be obtained from a wide variety of sources and altered so it is difficult to trace. In addition, as more producers gain access to tools that permit sophisticated editing, it will become more difficult to demonstrate when interview segments have been taken out of context and misrepresented. While this has always been an issue with the print media, the impression that one is actually hearing a person making a statement reinforces the credibility of audio sources for many listeners. As DAWs proliferate, we may be faced with a need for additional broadcasting courses in media literacy and production ethics.

Bibliography

Ely, M. (1995, February). Synchronizing digital audio to video. *Broadcast Engineering, 37* (2), 36-38, 47.

Hunold, K. (1996, April). Interfacing digital audio. *Broadcast Engineering, 38* (4), 80-88.

Nelson, M. (1995). *The cutting edge of audio production & audio post-production.* White Plains, NY: Knowledge Industry Publications.

Peterson, G. (1996). SADiE. Master system. [On-line]. Available: http://www.mixmag.com.

Pizzi, S. (1996a). Rededicating the DAW. *Broadcast Engineering, 38* (8), 72-73.

Pizzi, S. (1996b). Understanding audio data compression. *Broadcast Engineering, 38* (5), 52-60.

R&R Digital Guide, 1995. (1995). R&R: Author.

Reist, N. (1992, February 5). Live "Dead" broadcast goes digital. *Radio World*, 1, 11.

Reist, N. (1994a, January 12). Symphony recorded for radio broadcast. *Radio World*, 1, 12.

Reist, N. (1994b, December 14). Plug-and-play devices turn PCs into editors. *Radio World*, 13-14.

Skywalker Sound. (1996). [On-line]. Available: http://www.lum.com/thx/skywalker/
skywalker.html.

Sonic in the news. (1996). [On-line]. Available: http://www.sonic.com.

Trubitt, R. (1996). Head to head: Four digital audio workstations. In *Hyperstand.* [On-line]. Available: http://www.hyperstand.com/NewMedia/96/04/td/audio/
Digital_Audio_Workstations.html.

5

Audio Mixers, Processors, and Microphones

Jeffrey S. Wilkinson

Radio equipment focuses on the shaping and transmitting of voice, music, and sound effects. The human voice is probably the most important of the three—without the voice, radio must rely on feeling. The ability to take the human voice and transduce it into electronic impulses that can then be shaped and manipulated enables broadcasters to communicate ideas, thoughts, and opinions. It is therefore important to remember the importance of the human voice in terms of what it brings to radio, audio, and broadcast communications.

The heart of every radio station is the chain represented by the microphone, the processor, and the mixer (see Figure 5.1).

Figure 5.1
Radio Audio Chain

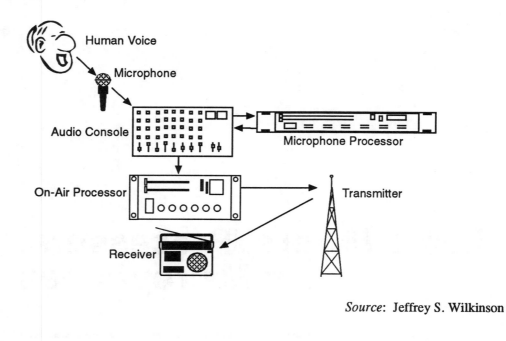

Source: Jeffrey S. Wilkinson

The Microphone

The microphone is the means by which the human voice is included in all audio production. Microphones come in a variety of shapes and sizes for a variety of applications, both in the field and in the studio. Costs of professional, low-impedance microphones can range from less than $100 to over $5,000. The most important decisions in selecting a microphone depend upon whether it will be used in the studio or in the field. Field microphones must be durable and portable, while studio microphones should aim for the highest quality. Most field microphones sell for under $300, studio microphones tend toward $400 to $600, with high-end microphones running into the thousands.

The Processor

A sound or signal *processor* is used to shape or alter the sound. There are four types of signal processors: those affecting spectrum, time, amplitude, and noise. An *equalizer* is an example of a spectrum processor. It allows an operator to enhance specified frequencies and/or mute others. A *delay* device affects time; when desired, audio can be stretched out or speeded up. A *compressor-limiter* affects the amplitude of the signal, perceived as making quiet segments louder and/or loud segments quieter. Finally, Dolby or DBX are two examples of *noise* processors. They identify and eliminate hiss, hum, or other unwanted noise. All of these devices are used to color the signal in some way that conveys the desired message or feeling.

In practice, there are two primary classes of processors:

- Those used to shape the on-air signal.

- Those used to shape sound in the production studio.

Shaping the on-air signal is important because what is broadcast must conform to basic laws of physics and engineering.

If the dynamic range of the broadcast signal is too broad, listeners quickly tire of constantly adjusting the volume. This may be evidenced on classical music stations, as orchestras alternate between extremes. Conversely, if the dynamic range is too narrow, listeners feel assaulted in the same way some TV commercials irritate with a barrage of words, music, etc. at a consistently high-volume level.

The processors used in a studio tend to be less expensive and more varied in their application. On-air processors typically cost several thousand dollars, while their studio counterparts can cost as little as a few hundred dollars.

The Audio Console

The audio console (also called a "board" and sometimes referred to as a mixer) allows the amplification, routing, and mixing of a variety of audio signals. The key elements to any mixer depend upon knowing what you wish to do with it. Mixers come in a variety of configurations and capabilities; it is up to you, the buyer, to decide what is best for your operation.

Mixers operate with three basic systems: input, output, and monitor. *Input* is the process of connecting signals from devices such as a microphone, CD player, tape deck, etc. to the console. The *output* system takes the mixed signal and routes it out to another device, such as a recording device or line to the transmitter for broadcast. The *monitor* system controls what is heard through headphones or monitor loudspeakers (see Figure 5.2).

Figure 5.2
Audio Console Signal Paths

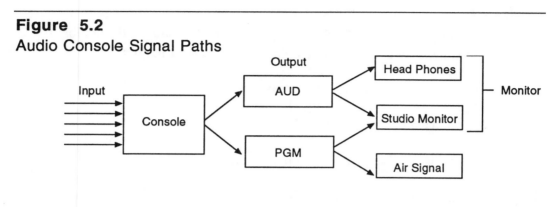

Source: Jeffrey S. Wilkinson

Analog consoles range from small, portable two- and four-channel mixers (for sports and sales remotes) for under $300, to custom-designed multi-channel digital stereo consoles that can cost over $100,000. Studio boards tend to run a dozen channels or so, and the production room boards may go to 12 to 24 channels, depending on the facility.

Background

The technology to convert the human voice into electronic signals was first developed nearly a century ago, with the first microphones making their appearance in the 1920s (Gross, 1997; Alten, 1994). The microphone has always been the primary piece of equipment used to capture and reproduce the human voice.

Throughout the century, microphones have typically been classified by use, internal construction, and/or element pickup pattern. Professional microphones have one of four types of elements in the head which changes acoustic energy into electrical energy. These elements are called moving coil (dynamic), ribbon, printed ribbon, and capacitor (condenser). Dynamic and condenser are labels held over from earlier days.

Moving coil microphones are the most common. They are durable and have a moving diaphragm inside that reverberates according to the sound reaching it.

Ribbon microphones are less common, but they are still in use. In the early days of radio, ribbon microphones were popular because of their "warm" reproduction of the human voice. Because they were so fragile (relying on a very thin metal ribbon that easily broke), however, ribbon microphones lost popularity. Manufacturers have since redesigned them, placing a shorter, longitudinally-placed ribbon in a stronger casing to make it more durable. Beyerdynamic makes a line of newer ribbon microphones which are fairly popular with broadcasters.

The printed ribbon microphone is also called a "regulated-phase" microphone. It is similar to a regular ribbon microphone, but considerably more durable. According to Alten (1994), a printed ribbon microphone has the best qualities of dynamic and ribbon microphones.

The capacitor microphone is a type of microphone that needs an external power source (such as a battery). There are several types of capacitor microphones that are very popular with broadcasters. The most popular microphone for television—the lavaliere—for example, is typically battery-powered. Much of the research and development regarding microphones seems to have been in the area of capacitor microphones. These types of microphones tend to be designed for a specific purpose, and have very sharply defined pickup patterns. Some of them are used in specific news and/or sports assignments (shotgun, parabolic, wireless, or boundary). A shotgun microphone, for example, allows one to record sound from quite a distance away. More than one unwitting city council member has been surprised to find out a reporter picked up whispered comments using this type of extremely directional microphone!

A final specialized type of condenser microphone is the boundary microphone. Crown International's PZM (pressure zone microphone) has been so popular that many believe PZM is the name of this particular type of microphone rather than a single brand (Compesi & Sherriffs, 1994). Boundary microphones are typically used in teleconferencing and for amplifying audiences. They tend to be physically flat and square, circular, or rectangular in shape. Boundary microphones are often used in difficult recording situations because they eliminate the problem of direct versus reflected sound waves. The "hollow echo" sound is avoided by a design that positions the pickup in such a way that the reflected and direct sound waves reach the pickup at the same time.

Processors

Sound processors have been around as long as radio. Since radio has become a medium for the masses and embraced music, the importance of sound processing has increased. Since the 1950s, Top 40 "screamer" DJs have known the importance of compressing/limiting the signal to maintain their high-energy sound and image. As radio has matured, however, a key selling point for on-air signal processors today is the ability to keep the signal within a range that does not cause listener fatigue.

Consoles

The audio console is the mainstay for the radio station or production facility. In terms of appearance, the biggest ergonomic development in the past few years is the decline of the rotary volume control (also known as a "pot"—short for "potentiometer"). Rotary pots have mostly been replaced by boards featuring the fader. The disappearance of rotary pots was apparently more a product of preference than anything else. One distributor lamented that younger broadcasters shun rotary pots because they simply "look old."

Modern consoles come in three basic types: analog, digital, and virtual. Analog consoles are the traditional multi-channel boards that have been in use since the beginning of broadcasting. The input devices are typically hard-wired (once a CD player is set up on channel 3, it stays on channel 3), but some models are now push-button assignable allowing an operator to reroute input devices onto any available channel. Typical broadcast boards contain eight to 12 channels in the on-air studio and 12 to 24 channels in the production studio. Production boards may also take advantage of automation features that allow the grouping of several signals at once.

Digital boards are relatively new on the scene. They tend to be a bit more expensive, and they are designed to have the "look and feel" of an analog board. Digital consoles typically have more flexibility in routing and processing signals, can be more streamlined in their design, and may have the capability of eliminating distortion and noise from the system.

The third type of console is the so-called "virtual console." Virtual consoles are basically a hard-disk computer system integrated into an audio production facility. The computer monitor displays a typical console—faders, processors, etc.—and the operator uses a mouse to operate the controls. The number of channels available is determined by the capacity of the hard disk. The virtual console is used primarily as an editor at this point. It is not typically used either as a studio console or a primary production console.

Recent Developments

Microphones

There have not been great changes in microphone technology. Microphone choice still seems to come down to taste and prior experience. One distributor likened it to "a classic case of Ford versus Chevy; most people still pick the microphone they've gotten used to." Nevertheless, there are some dominant brands of both studio and field microphones.

The most popular field microphones are the 635A line from ElectroVoice. Although essentially the same microphone, this model now comes in various colors, including a long-shank model. They generally list at $150, with typical discounting lowering the price to around $110 to $120. EV also makes an RE-50 microphone, which is a 635A inside another microphone housing with insulation/padding in between. The RE-50 runs around $250 list ($200 on the street).

Shure Brothers competes with the VP 64 which has proven to be very popular thanks to intense marketing. It is an inexpensive microphone ($135 list, $90 actual) that performs adequately in the field. A third popular field microphone is the AKG DE58E ($169).

In terms of studio microphones, the big three are the EV RE-20 ($655 list), its upgrade, the RE-27 N/D ($744 list), the Shure SM7 (list $566, actual $340), and the Sennheiser MD421 ($485/$399). For very deep pockets, the Neumann line can put you in the $1,000 to $2,500 range.

Digital Consoles

In the small, but growing, arena of digital consoles, Harris Corporation is establishing itself as a leader. Harris is aggressively touting its DRC 1000—Digital Radio Console. Billed as "the first digital console developed for radio broadcasts," this board (base price $16,000 to $18,000; with add-ons, it can go higher) was in use in 30 markets by early 1997. Facilities using the DRC 1000 are scattered among small, medium, and large markets.

The Harris DRC-1000. Photo courtesy of Harris Corporation.

The DRC-1000 has 11 asignable digital stereo inputs, five-band parametric equalization, one-touch stop/start buttons, and the capability of being upgraded to almost any size and/or configuration. The DRC-1000 allows a station to store board settings for each operator either on a card or using the internal memory. This allows each operator to instantly configure the layout of the console for their own show or production. The board itself is designed to appear like a traditional analog console so as to make learning easier. Finally, this board can operate either as an on-air or production board, and Harris says they hope to be able to network consoles within a facility in the future.

Other companies in the digital console business include the always-popular Wheatstone (which introduced the D-500 in 1996), Studer (D940 console), Fidelipac, and Logitek. Fidelipac has introduced an eight-input digital console ($11,000 to $12,000) which was first shipped to mostly larger markets in 1997. Likewise, Logitek has begun offering a digital console ($10,000 to $12,000), but, as of publication, has not moved any units into the field.

Analog Consoles

Wheatstone is a very popular supplier of broadcast consoles, and offers two lines. Wheatstone brand consoles are the "Cadillac" of consoles, and typically are not found in radio stations because the price tag can run between $20,000 and $100,000. Large market TV stations and major audio production facilities are the primary market for these.

For radio stations, Wheatstone Audioarts boards are common. Although the brand numbers seem to change frequently, the current R-line brand of Wheatstone Audioarts consoles range from a few thousand to over ten thousand dollars. The R-16, for example, is designed as an on-air board for small market radio stations, schools, and newsrooms. Recent list prices are $2,695 for the six-channel model and $3,895 for the 10-channel board.

The R-60 line of Wheatstone Audioarts boards range from $4,695 (12 mixer mainframe with eight mixers and six blanks for inputs or accessories) to $9,195 (18 mixer mainframe with 18 mixers and two blanks for mixers and accessories).

Pacific Recorders is fairly new to the game and is proving to be quite popular. The X-class line of consoles tend toward the expensive side ($20,000 to $40,000), but are becoming common in large markets. Pacific Recorders also offers a "radiomixer" and "productionmixer" for radio stations. Radiomixer is available in 12, 20, and 28 channel models.

In terms of mid-level audio consoles (both in price and capability), Broadcast Electronics has two lines, both of which are analog boards and continue to sell well. There are no immediate plans for BE to manufacture digital consoles.

Broadcast Electronics offers two lines: the AIR TRAK 90 and the Mix Trak 100. The AIR TRAK 90 runs from a six-channel board ($5,295) to a 24-channel model ($12,695). The Mix Trak 100 boards (12, 18, and 21 channels) start with the mainframe ($5,550 to $7,500), and then with add-ons, cards, and peripherals, the average cost runs around $15,000.

For radio production rooms, Mackie brand boards are very popular, although the vast array of knobs can be daunting for many. Mackie boards are compact, relatively inexpensive, and versatile. Many of their boards are listed with the "VLZ" suffix—very low impedance or "super quiet" in terms of unwanted line noise. The 16-channel CR1604VLZ is quite common in many radio production rooms, with a list price of $1,099. A compact model, the MS1202VLZ Audio Mixer, is a budget-minded eight-channel (with rotary knobs) production mixer for a few hundred dollars. Autogram, Yamaha, and Arrakis are also popular brands and can be found in many radio stations.

Dynamax (owned by Fidelipac) makes a couple of mid-priced consoles, depending on whether you want three inches between faders (the six-channel board runs around $3,500, and the 12-channel goes around $5,500) or two inches (the 10-channel board is $5,000, and the 18 channel board is $7,200). Radio Systems RS consoles (six channels, $4,795; 24 channels, $12,995) are popular with broadcasters, as are Soundcraft DLX (eight channels, $4490; 32 channels, $11,950) consoles.

Analog boards tend to be much less expensive than their digital counterparts. A digital console that sells for $12,000 typically has an analog counterpart for $9,000 or less. The decision to buy analog or digital technology depends on the needs of the facility. On-air boards are now desired to be "idiot proof"; station managers want on-air console operation to be virtually thought-free. This is not a disparaging view of today's announcers; it is the realization that on-air personalities are most effective when they don't have to bother with complex banks of knobs and switches.

Production consoles are a different story. For high quality and maximum flexibility, these boards must be more complex in order to attempt ambitious audio productions. This means having multi-track stereo capabilities with every type of studio sound processor possible.

Processors

On-Air Signal Processors

There are roughly a dozen on-air processors on the market. The leader and most popular with broadcasters are those from Orban. The Optimod models come in various sizes in both analog and digital configurations. The digital 8200 is the luxury model, while the 2200 is economy class. The analog version (8100) continues to sell well and remains popular with broadcasters.

The 8200 digital audio processor is a complete digital audio processing system containing almost any feature you want. It has several factory presets, as well as up to 32 custom presets. Depending on whether you purchase the two-band or the multi-band version, your price will run from $7,000 to $11,000.

Cutting Edge manufactures the Unity 2000I FM stereo processor. Typical functions offered by these units include selectable broadband AGC (automatic gain control), selectable phase rotator, adjustable bass enhancer, adjustable crossovers, four band processor/leveler, four band limiter, clipper/low pass filter system, stereo generator, and selectable composite processor. Nine factory presets are included; you may create up to 50 of your own. Its list price is in the $8,500 range. Other features include comprehensive front panel metering, four level security, day-part processing, and an RS-232 port for computer control from virtually anywhere.

Gentner offers the Prism II FM. This compressor "expands only when necessary" so as not to irritate listeners. This processor operates in four bands: low, mid, presence, and high, each with independent circuitry. Audio in one band can be adjusted, then added back to the final mix. A "mix level" control for each band allows you to set the percentage of each band you want in the final mix, and a single "density" control adjusts the total amount of processing action. Increased density will result in a loud, aggressive signal, while lower settings will give you an open, natural sound.

Voice Processors

Microphone processors are very common. The field is currently dominated by three companies: Symmetrix, Orban, and Air Corporation. In small and medium markets, the Symmetrix 528 and, more recently, the 528E microphone processors are common. They list at $700 and retail around $550. In medium and large markets, the Orban 787 is very common. There are a variety of configurations you can get, but the basic unit lists between $1,450 and $1,750. A third processor that finds favor with broadcasters is by Air Corporation. It is priced around $800, with the actual street price a little less ($750).

Factors to Watch

Microphones

Microphone manufacturing appears to be very stable. Most microphone manufacturers and broadcasters are sticking with what has worked for them in the past. Despite rumors, the possibility of a "digital microphone" is *not* on the horizon. JVC has experimented with digital microphones, but they have not caught on with broadcasters. A digital microphone is really a standard microphone with an analog-to-digital converter housed inside the microphone stem. The signal coming out of the microphone is digital and is then routed to (presumably) a digital audio console. Because of their newness and the coveted "digital" label, you would pay more for these microphones with little to show for it. The specifications for high-end analog microphones are extremely high, and no one has plans to develop the digital larynx that would complete the "digital" chain.

Processors

Broadcasters are continuing to embrace a small number of processors to shape and alter sound. The majority of processors being used are still analog, but the shift toward digital is remaining gradual but strong. Expect the strong companies to continue; DBX (voice processor), for example, is owned by Orban (voice and on-air processors) which, in turn, is owned by Harmon International. Harmon International also owns AKG (microphones), JBL (speakers), Soundcraft (boards), and others. The relatively small number of players is not expected to change too much.

Consoles

Digital boards, so far, have not proven to be wildly successful on-air boards; Harris, Fidelipac, and Logitek make them, but the price has made some balk. In terms of production studios, digital boards show some success. The Yamaha Promix series has been mentioned, but this is still in its infancy. The primary engineering concerns with digital boards are with:

(1)   Varying sample rate conversions between the board and outboard equipment devices.

(2)   Integrating analog equipment into a digital configuration (Berry, T., chief engineer, WUOT-FM, personal conversation, January 8, 1997).

The main point for broadcasters to remember is that analog audio consoles are better than ever for a lower price. A good mid-line console generally can run $6,000 to $8,000 with more peripherals, more variability, and better specifications than 10 years ago. Even with inflation, the list price on many consoles has not changed in the past few years.

Overall, the industry is in the beginning of an interim stage between analog and digital. There are plenty of older broadcasters who like and are used to analog in-board equipment. Over time, the demand for digital hardware will increase as the next generation of broadcasters becomes more comfortable with computers and digital technology.

Bibliography

Adams, M. H., & Massey, K. K. (1995). *Introduction to radio: Production and programming*. Madison, WI: Brown & Benchmark.

Alten, S. (1994). *Audio in media* (4th ed.). Belmont, CA: Wadsworth.

Compesi, R. J., & Sherriffs, R. E. (1994). *Video field production and editing* (3rd ed.). Boston: Allyn and Bacon.

Console technology evolves at NAB. (1996, May 29). *Radio World*, 44-45.

Gross, L. S. (1997). *Telecommunications: An introduction to electronic media* (6th ed.). Madison, WI: Brown & Benchmark.

Harris DRC 1000. (1997, January 3). [On-line]. Available: http://www.broadcast. harris.com/audiometrics/drc1000.html.

O'Donnell, L. B., Benoit, P., & Hausman, C. (1993). *Modern radio production* (3rd ed.). Belmont, CA: Wadsworth.

III

Video Production Technologies

J ust as audio production has been transformed by digital technology, so has the production environment for video producers. In some ways, this transformation is going to be even more dramatic due to the decision by the FCC to mandate a national conversion to a digital transmission system over the coming decade. While the basic elements of the broadcast production, transmission, and reception triad may be a mixture of analog and digital technologies during this transition, the trend is clearly toward an entirely digital signal path early in the next century.

This section examines the fundamental elements of video production from the camera lens to the digital server that feeds edited programming to the transmitter. While the focus is on the impact of digital technology on video production, we have also included information on recent developments in such vital areas as television lighting. The availability of new fluorescent and lightweight HMI lighting instruments may have as great an impact on the look of television programs as the introduction of high-definition images. All of the developments in the area of video production are intertwined—as we move toward the introduction of high-definition digital cameras, technologies must be developed for the recording and non-linear editing of these images. The entire signal chain will need to be reinvented as broadcast stations across North America convert from NTSC to digital broadcasting. The purpose of this section is to examine each area in light of recent technological developments and to consider important factors to watch as the national broadcast conversion begins.

Chapter 6 reviews new developments in camera and lens technology. With the forthcoming conversion to widescreen digital production, producers will need to consider purchasing cameras that are capable of capturing both conventional 4:3 images as well as 16:9 high-definition material. As these multi-format HDTV cameras decline in price, television viewers can expect to see more prime-time imagery shot on digital videotape rather than film. The chapter also addresses innovative digital circuitry in new cameras that can smooth out facial lines or electronically dampen camera vibration in handheld shots.

Chapter 7 provides a thorough analysis of the wealth of videotape formats presently available to broadcast producers. Tables of analog and digital tape formats are provided to simplify comparisons of 23 distinct systems used in contemporary professional television production. The author provides a detailed analysis of new compact digital video production formats such as DVCPRO and DVCAM, which are making inroads in the fields of news and documentary production long dominated by Betacam. Producers have never had such a wide variety of formats to choose from, and this chapter will assist in sorting out the pros and cons of the various systems.

Chapter 8 looks at a new technology that has spread like wildfire through the broadcast television community—the video server. While digital hard disks have been a familiar storage device in computers for decades, until recently it was impossible to find one that could serve digital video in real time that met broadcast standards. Since 1995, however, they have become commonplace at the local and national level for news production, on-air program playback, and video-on-demand systems. Broadcasters and cable operators are looking at server systems as a potential replacement for cart machines, as they have far fewer moving parts and offer non-linear access to any material stored within. Students and professionals alike need to understand the potential of server technology as more and more of these digital systems are used for the production and playback of television programming.

Linear editing technology is the subject of Chapter 9. To paraphrase a classic Mark Twain line, "rumors of its death are premature." Linear videotape will be a mainstay in the broadcast production environment for the indefinite future, and this chapter examines both analog and digital linear editing technologies. It explains the benefits and drawbacks of both systems, and why manufacturers continue to introduce new linear editing systems as a bridge from the analog systems of the present day to new digital formats such as Digital-S and DV that are just now coming on-line.

Chapter 10 reviews the present status of non-linear editing equipment, a rapidly-shifting target. Record numbers of new non-linear systems were introduced at the annual NAB show in 1996. This chapter outlines the significant advantages non-linear editing offers to video producers despite the added time needed to digitize analog footage. These systems are proliferating in every area of video post-production, and this chapter provides the basic knowledge needed by producers of all experience levels.

Lest we forget any of the broadcasting hardware essential in switching and manipulating video signals, Chapter 11 looks at the state of the art in switchers, digital video effects (DVE) devices, and new digital signal processors. This chapter reviews the evolution of the broadcast production switcher from a simple device that cuts between studio cameras to large digital, multibus, multi-effect systems that seamlessly blend all the visual program elements together.

Last, but certainly not least in the eyes of the editors, is Chapter 12 on lighting technology. As noted earlier, creating quality television lighting is a crucial part of the production process, and this chapter examines several evolutionary technologies that have transformed the way television productions look. To appreciate the difference, one only has to see the effect of soft fluorescent lighting on Peter Jennings on ABC's *World News Tonight* and compare it with the harsh, high-intensity lighting of NBC's *Huntley-Brinkley Report* from the 1960s.

This section on video production technologies provides a comprehensive look at the dramatic progress that has been made in the past 10 years in reducing the size of production hardware while simultaneously improving the image quality seen by the viewer. Any producer who remembers shooting with a heavy three-tube camera and an attached U-Matic portapak (compared with a lightweight DV camcorder) will attest that the new digital formats have much to offer in addition to better image quality.

6

Television Cameras and Lenses

David Sedman

As noted in Chapter 2, the television broadcast industry is undergoing a major transition from an analog-transmitted medium to a more dynamic digital medium. Much of the discussion about digital television concerns the cost and size of television sets and the implementation of service by broadcasters. However, the most intriguing advances in research and development involve video cameras and lenses. This is logical, since the camera has always been at the center of the evolutionary development of television technology. The look of every contemporary situation comedy, televised sporting event, on-scene video expos, and live traffic shot is dependent on the type of camera and lens selected for use. Some might think of the camera as the "passive observer" in the production process. However, contemporary broadcast cameras have an array of new features that assist broadcast producers. An understanding of the changes in camera design allows one to comprehend the general evolution of television technology.

Background

The roots of television camera history can be traced back to the 19th century; however, its development began in the 20th century. One of the major goals in the creation of television was to produce a camera that had acceptable resolution. The first cameras used mechanical scanning which had a resolution of less than 250 lines per frame. Vladimir Zworykin, generally considered the founder of the television camera, invented the iconoscope in 1923 (Sterling & Head, 1990). The iconoscope was the first electronic camera pickup tube and was used in the television experiments of the 1920s and 1930s. During this timeframe, engineering teams were able to double the lines of resolution in the electronic television system.

Television equipment left the confines of the laboratory in 1939 when RCA introduced television to the public during the New York World's Fair. Television cameras documented fair events in live telecasts that led to great interest in the technology. Two years later, the Federal Communications Commission (FCC) adopted a modified black-and-white TV system with 525 lines per frame at 30 frames per second (Sterling & Head, 1990). In the 1950s, the FCC adopted a color system using the same 525 scan-line standard. This standard, named NTSC for the National Television System Committee, became the predominant television transmission standard for the balance of the 20th century in the United States.

Although the transmission system remained unchanged, a number of advances introduced over the past 35 years have improved the nature of television cameras and lenses. The studio camera was the first type of camera invented. These cameras are mounted on rolling pedestals and used for in-studio productions and major remote telecasts, such as football games and political rallies. The development of field lenses with zoom ranges up to 70× helped give home viewers the clichéd "best seat in the house." The cameras, lenses, and pedestals were, however, too bulky for certain events.

Thus, spot coverage of news and other field production was generally captured on film until the beginning of the 1970s.

The development of portable videotape formats helped lead to the electronic field production (EFP) and electronic news gathering (ENG) revolution of the 1970s. However, other innovations helped bring about this change. Lightweight ENG/EFP lenses with limited zoom ranges ensured that the camera was not front-heavy. As for cameras, the increased use of transistors and semiconductors made them lighter and more durable.

The evolution of cameras is best exemplified by the image sensors used in their construction. The image-sensing device is an element in the camera which converts light into electricity. The two major categories of image sensors are the pickup tube and the chip or CCD (charge-coupled device). Cameras are designed with one, two, or three image sensors. The goal of broadcast engineers is to deliver high-quality, *component* video information that keeps the red, green, and blue color information separated. A three-tube or three-chip camera delivers superior picture quality because separate sensors are dedicated to the red, green, and blue signals. Thus, the majority of cameras purchased by broadcast stations have three image sensors.

Cameras with one image sensor combine the luminance or "Y" signal and chrominance or "C" signal into one *composite* signal. Although these cameras do not deliver a "broadcast-quality" picture, they are generally the smallest and least expensive type of camera. The one-chip camera is generally aimed at the consumer camcorder market. However, some broadcasters have adapted one-chip cameras as miniature surveillance cameras used in undercover news reporting.

The rarest type of camera features two image sensors. These cameras separate the Y and C signals. As the "middle grade" of camera, they suffer from being too expensive for most consumers and not of high enough quality for most broadcasters.

Prior to the 1980s, a camera's image sensing device was some type of pickup tube. The most common tubes were the Plumbicon and the Saticon. Tube cameras were susceptible to damage from bright lights and were rather fragile. Further, the camera tubes had to be "registered" before every use, i.e., the pickup tubes had to be aligned to deliver a clear and accurate signal.

As such, they frequently needed attention from engineers to ensure picture quality. The chip camera emerged as the prevalent camera type because it is more durable and requires less maintenance than tube cameras. The quality and reliability of three-chip cameras has reached such a high level that some stations have a secondary studio space with cameras which are used both in the studio and as field units.

Recent Developments

According to a 1996 survey of chief engineers, 23% of stations reserved a portion of their budget for ENG/EFP cameras, 19% bought lenses, and 7% purchased studio cameras (Silbergleid, 1996). Stations devoted an average of $56,500 toward EFP/ENG cameras, almost $20,000 for lenses, and about $625,000 for studio cameras. Seemingly with each passing year, the cameras and lenses adopted by broadcasters offer new features and allow greater flexibility. Two general categories that cover contemporary technological trends in the area of television cameras and lenses are digital circuitry and automation/robotics.

Digital Circuitry

Cameras with digital circuitry are able to perform functions once reserved for other stages of the production process. Chip cameras allow for storage and manipulation of the pixels that comprise the image. The first digital effects included freeze frames, strobing, dissolves, and digital zooms. Prior to the introduction of chip cameras, effects such as these could only be achieved during post-production.

While broadcasters rarely used these early digital effects, subsequent features were more valuable. Imagine having a field shoot where the talent has noticeable facial wrinkles. To smooth the wrinkles without sacrificing image sharpness would require lighting changes, additional makeup, or even a post-production touch-up. A number of professional cameras have skin tone detail functions. The camera's normal detail or DTL function would allow for a sharper picture, but would also emphasize wrinkles and imperfections on the talent's face. The skin tone detail automatically detects skin tone elements and prevents DTL from being applied in those areas. The result is a sharp picture without harsh facial blemishes. The inventor of this skin detail circuitry won an Emmy Award, and the feature is used in many contemporary studio cameras.

The combination of a camera's freeze and superimpose feature has aided in the area of continuity. If the director has established a scene and needs to reshoot an element of that scene later, the last frame of the scene can be called up and superimposed over live video. The props and talent in the scene can then be reset in their exact positions. In addition, some cameras will recall all of the set-up parameters from the previous shot and automatically re-establish them for the current videography. Therefore, the camera has assisted in continuity and with the engineering aspects of the production.

If a videographer is nervous or if the camera is being shaken slightly by vibrations from a crowd, the on-air result can be unsettling to the home viewer. Many professional lenses are now being made with image stabilizers, or they can be equipped with image stabilizer adapters. The image stabilizer works with a vari-angle prism that bends the angle of the light to compensate for the vibration of the camera. Unfortunately, the creation of a long-range telephoto lens with image stabilization is not currently feasible (Haigney, 1996). Advances in digital or electronic stabilization may make this a reality. Digital stabilization extracts a small portion of the video data from around the edges of a shot and attempts to compensate for the camera's shaky motion. Thus, the camera or its lens may be serving as an internal "steadicam" for the videographer.

One of the most ambitious digital cameras is the CamCutter developed by Ikegami and Avid Technology in 1995. The CamCutter is a tapeless camera that records information onto a computer disk. The camera offers a variety of intriguing features. It can record continuously in 60-second intervals. The videographer is able to preserve the best shots and free the remainder of the drive for new footage. The videographer can then edit the entire project and output it live on-the-air from the camera. An entire project can be kept in a digital format and the camera itself is the production and post-production center. With the sweeping features brought about by digital technology, cameras have become much more than "passive observers."

The CamCutter is a tapeless camera designed for digital news gathering. Photo courtesy of Ikegami and Avid.

Automation/Robotics

As is the case in many industries, technological advances may bring some degree of automation. The broadcast industry has its share of production tasks assisted by automation, including master control and camera operation. As noted, engineers are no longer needed to provide daily registration of cameras or to be on hand to reset video controls for given scenes. Instead, the camera can store set-up information almost automatically. All one needs is the camera operator and, depending on the production situation, even that job can be automated.

The adoption rate of robotic studio pedestals and short-arm jibs (such as those attached to goal posts in football telecasts) continues to rise. A number of factors suggest that robotic pedestals will continue to replace human operators in studio and remote settings. The robotic mount has numerous advantages. Some robotic systems can store more than 1,000 combinations of movements while controlling eight different cameras. Removing the human operator allows directors to place cameras virtually anywhere they desire. Heading into the 21st century, camera bodies continue to become more compact. With this miniaturization comes a number of smaller accessories, lenses, and pedestals. Since smaller pedestals can be more challenging for people to operate than the larger units, a director may find that robotic operators are superior to humans.

The increased use of helicopter footage by news departments is also being assisted by automation. A camera is attached directly to the helicopter, and an operator uses a joystick to control it. Camera shots are enhanced by a powered zoom lens with image stabilization. One system, called GryoCam, can rotate 360° and also provide relatively clear and stable shots of people on the ground.

Of course, an operator must see the action to provide viewers with the best shot. There are cameras in use by broadcasters, however, which can detect images that the human eye and conventional camera cannot. These cameras operate on the principle of infrared (IR) imaging. IR imaging is dependent on heat, not reflected light. As a result, IR cameras are able to operate in total darkness. While the most memorable IR shots were seen during Operation Desert Storm, broadcasters have begun to adopt this technology for around-the-clock sky coverage of everything from chases to natural disasters (Bell, 1996). A traffic helicopter can be equipped with a dual camera system to take normal video during the day and IR shots at night.

Factors to Watch

The Transformation to Digital Television

With more than 1,500 television stations and scores of cable television networks in the United States making the conversion to digital transmission, new cameras and lenses will be purchased in record numbers. This conversion brings with it some relatively new terms such as "down-conversion" and "up-conversion." Down-conversion will reformat 16 × 9 HDTV images to a 4 × 3 NTSC aspect ratio. With many network series already being shot in widescreen and converted to 4 × 3, this process should be undetectable. The more noticeable change will concern up-converting camera images from NTSC to HDTV. The current up-conversion technology produces less-than-satisfactory results. Therefore, broadcasters will undoubtedly look at up-converting their NTSC cameras as a temporary fix, at best.

Many contemporary lenses, including the one above, are designed to be compatible with both the 4:3 and 16:9 aspect ratios. Photo courtesy of Fujinon.

Greater detail captured by cameras brings new problems to set designers. Small imperfections or markings on set pieces previously hidden by the technical limitations of the equipment will now be more apparent. Set design shortcuts, such as painted plastic or Styrofoam, were ideal for the NTSC system. These techniques will not provide satisfactory results in the realm of HDTV. Hence, along with the conversion costs of hardware will come additional production costs. Network executives have estimated these additional costs to be in the 25% to 30% range.

HDTV cameras are being developed to bring the quality of video closer to that of film. During the 1996-1997 television season, only 27% of network prime-time shows were shot on video (Oh, 1997). With many studios requiring two versions of their productions (a 4×3 version for current broadcasts and a 16×9 format for future syndication), film has a significant quality and flexibility advantage over NTSC video. The technology base is beginning to change. In 1997, Turner Broadcasting began using HDTV equipment in the production of a wildlife series, and Sony introduced its HD Betacam camcorder (Beacham, 1996). As high-definition cameras become more commonplace in the United States, costs for tape and cameras will continue to decrease. Therefore, another factor to watch will be a decreased reliance on film in episodic television program production.

Many video production facilities and television stations are adopting high-definition studio cameras like the one pictured here. Photo courtesy of Sony.

New Connections

In both studio and remote broadcasts, among the most familiar elements are the large reels of camera cable. The most common camera cables are copper-based. A factor to watch will be how the signal gets from the camera to its next destination. Television executives will invest a significant portion of their budgets to upgrade cameras and video switchers for the advanced TV system. It is likely that many stations will also consider installing fiber optic cable for improved performance. Fiber optic cable contains thin glass strands and can provide superior performance over long distances compared with copper cable.

Outside of the studio, the problems are more diverse. In live productions, wiring cameras to production trucks is still commonplace. Set-up time can be costly, and at least two people are needed to ensure that a signal is getting back to the station. Improvements in optical beam transmission are allowing videographers to send live shots to a microwave or satellite truck without the use of wires. The radius of contemporary optical beam transmitters is over 2.5 miles (Dickson, 1996). With fiber optic telephone lines, it is conceivable that videographers could routinely send live shots without cables to a dedicated phone line. The signals would be received by the station and transmitted live. In such a scenario, equipment costs, personnel, and set-up time would all be minimized.

A major problem for contemporary videographers and editors is the down-time associated with digitizing field tapes. The IEEE 1394 connection known as "FireWire" is a port that carries video, audio, and time code data from the camera (or digital recorder) to the non-linear editing workstation. This connector allows for dubbing of footage without generational loss. FireWire's transfer rate is four times real-time speed, which saves valuable time for both the personnel and the workstation. As broadcast technology moves toward the digital age, FireWire should become a very popular camera-editor connector.

Video cameras and lenses have been transformed from passive observers with minimal features and resolution, to a more vibrant production tool. Digital video cameras of today offer better resolution than one can see on any current NTSC television set. They allow users to get more automated assistance and set-up information than ever before. Top-quality cameras use miniature components which have made them more portable than their predecessors.

At present, the price of digital video cameras is high compared with older models; however, prices will decrease as more models become available. Digital video cameras can also be easily linked to, or become a part of, a computer system. All of these attributes are now being considered in the transition to advanced digital television technology in the United States.

New digital cameras at all price and performance levels will improve video image quality at a time when high-definition television will make it possible for viewers to actually perceive the improvement.

Bibliography

Beacham, F. (1996, December 13). Sony creates HDTV format for Betacam. *TV Technology*, 1, 10.

Bell, M. (1996, June). Camera technology heats up with infrared developments. *Television Broadcast*, 21, 24.

Dickson, G. (1996, March 18). Canon unveils improved optical system. *Broadcasting & Cable*, 59.

Haigney, K. (1996, April). What's your (focal) point? *Television Broadcast*, 60.

Oh, M. (1997, January). 1997 TV post-production guide. *Film and Video*, 50-56, 84-86.

Silbergleid, M. (1996, April). A billion dollar year for stations, budgets up 15 percent in broadcast. *Television Broadcast*, 1, 46-51.

Sterling, C. H., & Head, S. W. (1990). *Broadcasting in America*. Boston: Houghton Mifflin, 61, 62.

7

Videotape Formats

James C. Foust

Many of the most eagerly-anticipated innovations of the digital video age involve using new types of media to store video information. Once video is in digital form, it can be stored and retrieved using the same methods as digital audio or computer data. As a result, we are seeing digital video recorded on optical disks, tiny high-capacity hard drives, and even electronic chips. In a growing number of facilities, tape systems are being replaced by *video servers*, which store and deliver digital video via computer networks.

With all of the exciting possibilities of digital video, it may be tempting to dismiss videotape as a storage medium. However, videotape is adapting to the digital age as well, with new formats designed to integrate with computer systems and provide cost-effective acquisition and storage. In fact, so many new digital videotape formats are being introduced that there is fear in the industry of "format wars" among competing manufacturers. Indeed, the prospective digital videotape customer faces a dizzying array of choices, with no one format clearly superior to the others.

Tape has several advantages over other storage media, the most important of which is cost. While some tape formats allow several hours of video to be recorded on a single cassette, disk-based media have much more limited capacity. This translates into a significant cost differential; in some cases, storing video on tape costs less than one-tenth of what it costs to store on disk (McConnell, 1994). For instance, Avid's highly-touted CamCutter—a digital recording unit that transfers video directly to a hard disk—holds 20 minutes of video and sells for $19,000. For about $2,000 less, Panasonic offers a DVCPRO digital tape unit *and* camera that will record up to one hour of video (McConnell, 1995).

Tape also relies on proven technology. While the electronic circuitry used to record and play back digital video is quite different from that used to record analog, many formats have tape threading and transport systems that have been proven over many years. This means that the mechanical portions of tape systems are more easily maintained and, in many cases, less prone to failure than disk systems. As disk-based systems become more common in the marketplace and their mechanisms are tested and debugged in the field, this will become less of an issue. For now, however, the cost involved in maintaining disk-based systems can make tape very attractive (McConnell, 1994).

The most significant drawback to tape is its linear storage method. While disk- and chip-based media offer nearly instantaneous access to any portion of the stored material, a videotape must still be rewound or fast-forwarded to access different information. Although newer tape formats boast improved speed in rewinding, fast-forwarding, and shuttling, they are still not as convenient as nonlinear media. This means that videotape editing takes longer and does not offer the same "cut and paste" capabilities as non-linear systems.

This chapter presents an overview of videotape formats currently in use, concentrating on digital formats. It begins with a look back at analog formats, and then examines digital formats designed for high end, low end, and consumer use.

Background—Analog Recording Formats

At the 1956 National Association of Broadcasters (NAB) convention, the Ampex Corporation unveiled its VR-1000, the first commercial videotape recorder. The VR-1000 used four recording heads to record black-and-white video on two-inch-wide tape; thus, the format came to be called "quadruplex" or "quad." Two years later, RCA and Ampex added color capability to the format, and, in 1965, Ampex introduced *high-band color* in the VR-2000 recorder. High-band color, so named because it uses a higher carrier frequency, greatly improved the quality of color recording and quickly overtook existing low-band units (Inglis, 1990). Quadruplex became the standard of the broadcast industry, and remained dominant well into the 1970s (Noll, 1988). However, quadruplex's large tape, which was wound on spools and had to be threaded through the machine, made the design impractical for portable or small-scale applications.

During the 1960s, several companies experimented with *helical scan formats*. While quadruplex recorded short "tracks" perpendicularly across the tape, helical scan recorded at an angle. Thus, a single recording head could be used with narrower tape. Helical scan machines were also easier to maintain, and, by the mid-1970s, a number of companies were producing rival helical scan systems using one-inch-wide tape. The Society of Motion Picture and Television Engineers (SMPTE) initially gave Ampex's VPR-1 system status as the industry standard, granting it the "Type A" designation. However, rivals Sony and Bosch continued to push their incompatible systems. Finally, in 1977, SMPTE sanctioned a compromise standard between Sony and Ampex as "Type C," and designated a system produced by Bosch as "Type B" (Inglis, 1990).

Although one-inch machines were much smaller than two-inch units, neither format was particularly suited to field production. However, the U-Matic videotape recorder, introduced by Sony in 1972, made portable machines practical—although certainly not convenient by today's standards. The format, which uses 3/4-inch tape enclosed in cassettes, became the virtually unchallenged standard for field production and news until the 1980s and boasts an installed base of more than one million. In the face of newer, smaller, and higher-quality formats, U-Matic has remained a viable standard. "It just doesn't seem to want to go away," Sony's Joseph Tibensky recently remarked (Silbergleid, 1995, p. 1). In the consumer market, JVC's VHS (Video Home System) format, using 1/2-inch cassettes, has become the standard. Introduced in 1975, VHS vanquished a challenge from Sony's Betamax system to gain nearly complete control of the home market.

Aside from the Quad, U-Matic, and VHS formats, however, no other systems have achieved such dominant status as "standards." Type C has replaced quadruplex in most broadcast applications, and Sony's professional Betacam system is in widespread use in segments such as electronic news gathering (ENG), but most other formats have not been so universally accepted. Indeed, since Ampex debuted its videotape machine in 1956, at least 20 other videotape formats have been introduced in the United States (Chan, 1994). For the most part, each new format has been targeted at a particular segment of the video market, and the size of these segments has grown to the point that several formats have been able to flourish. In fact, some formats have even helped create markets, as was the case when JVC's S-VHS and Sony's Hi8 spawned the so-called "prosumer" market. These formats helped bridge the wide gap between professional and consumer video equipment, bringing high-quality, affordable video capabilities to a larger market. Table 7.1 lists some of the most popular analog tape formats.

Despite the great strides that have been made in analog videotape technology in the areas of price, size, and quality, the future undoubtedly belongs to digital formats. John Watkinson, a digital recording engineer, notes that analog recording has become a "mature technology" that has practically reached its limits. "The process of refinement produces increasingly small returns," he notes (Watkinson, 1992, p. 1).

For this reason, most manufacturers of video equipment have been concentrating on digital technology since the beginning of the decade. While early digital formats were aimed at high-end applications, in the past few years, digital technology has begun to "trickle down" as well to mid- and low-cost equipment.

Table 7.1

Analog Tape Formats

Format	Introduction	Tape Width	Applications
Quad	1956	2 inches	General purpose
A, B, C	1970s	1 inch	General purpose
U-Matic	1972	3/4 inch	Broadcast, post-production, industrial
U-Matic SP	1985	3/4 inch	Broadcast, post-production, industrial
Betacam	1982	1/2 inch	Broadcast, EFP/ENG, post-production, industrial
Betacam SP	1987	1/2 inch	High-end production, broadcast, EFP/ENG, industrial
VHS	1975	1/2 inch	Consumer, low-end production and distribution
MII	1985	1/2 inch	Broadcast, EFP/ENG, post-production
8mm	1984	8mm	Prosumer, industrial
S-VHS	1987	1/2 inch	Prosumer, EFP/ENG, industrial
Hi8	1988	8 mm	Prosumer, EFP/ENG, industrial

Source: James C. Foust

Digital Formats—Technical Considerations

While an in-depth discussion of the engineering considerations of digital video recording is beyond the scope of this chapter, it is necessary to review some technical information in order to understand the advantages and challenges of digital video.

Digital video, like any other data in digital form, is made up of binary strings of "off" and "on" signals. These signals are normally represented by "0" and "1," respectively, and, at any given moment, the value of a digital signal must be either "0" or "1." Analog information, on the other hand, is represented by "waves" that vary within a range of values. Analog information, such as sound or light waves, is converted to digital form through a process called *digitization*. In this process, the analog wave's value is checked—or *sampled*—many times each second. Each time the analog wave is sampled, its value is converted into binary form. Through this process, the information represented in the analog wave is converted into a digital *bitstream*.

Information in a digital bitstream is much less susceptible to interference and signal degradation than an analog signal. If you start with a U-Matic or VHS tape, make a copy of that tape, then a copy of the copy, and so on, you will notice that each copy, or *generation*, is of lower quality than the one that came before it. A typical analog recording, in fact, becomes practically unviewable after only a few generations. This is because the analog signal is degraded by interference and distortion during the recording process. Digital video, on the other hand, can be copied without such degradation. Although other factors prevent digital video formats from producing infinite generations of original quality, some digital systems can produce 30 generations without appreciable distortion (Chan, 1994).

Figure 7.1
"Generations" of Videotape

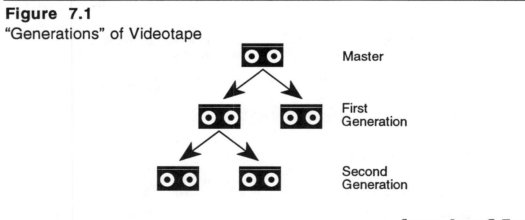

Source: James C. Foust

Each time a video- or audiotape is copied, a new generation is made. The original recording is known as the first generation, and a copy of that original is the second generation. Copies of the second generation become the third generation, and so on. You can make as many copies as you want of a first generation tape and all will be considered second generation, as long as all copies used the first-generation tape as the source.

Since the D-VHS recorder merely records a digital bitstream, it does no analog-to-digital conversion. Thus, it has no sampling rate. Another major advantage is that digital signals can be manipulated by a computer. Once converted to a digital bitstream, a computer treats digital video just like any other digital information. To a computer, there is really no difference between a bitstream that represents a word processing file and one that represents a clip of digital video. To be sure, the digital video bitstream represents a far greater amount of information, as discussed in the next section, but with a powerful enough computer, digital video can be edited with the same ease as words in a term paper or numbers on a spreadsheet.

Digital video images represent a very large amount of data. A single frame of digitized video can contain more than 750 kilobytes of information, enough to fill more than half of a high-density floppy disk. Since there are 30 frames in each second of video, it can take about 1.3 *giga*bytes to store one minute's worth of digital video (Rubin, 1991). Because digital video is dynamic (it changes 30 times each second), this information must be moved quickly in order to maintain an uninterrupted picture. Thus, transmitting digital video—from a videotape to a disk, for example—requires a method with high *bandwidth*. Bandwidth is a measure of electrical capacity, much as the diameter of a pipe determines how much water can flow through it.

The most common method of dealing with these storage and bandwidth demands is through a process called *compression*, which reduces the size of the video bitstream. A number of compression standards have been developed, each targeted at a specific application. MPEG-1 compression, for example, is designed to compress video for use on CD-ROMs, while MPEG-2 is designed for broadcast applications. All compression methods work by analyzing video information and converting it into a less data-intensive form. *Lossless* compression methods do not reduce the quality of the video signal, while *lossy* methods do (Van Tassel, 1996).

The sampling rate can also affect the size of the video bitstream. A color video signal is made up of two types of information: *luminance* (brightness) and *chrominance* (color). In a *component* video system, the luminance and chrominance information are kept separated, with luminance contained in one "channel" and chrominance information contained in two other channels. In a system with a 4:2:2 sampling rate, the luminance information is sampled 13.5 million times a second, and each of the chrominance channels are sampled 6.75 million times a second. A 4:1:1 system samples each chrominance channel at half the rate of the 4:2:2 system (Paulson, 1996). All else being equal, a higher sampling rate leads to higher storage and bandwidth requirements, but it can produce a higher-quality picture.

A *composite* video system combines the luminance and chrominance information onto one channel. While more susceptible to some kinds of distortion than component systems, composite systems require less sophisticated circuitry and less bandwidth (Inglis, 1993). Until recently, in fact, the technology to record in digital component format was prohibitively expensive for all but high-end systems. Today, component technology has developed to a degree that even low-cost digital systems use it. It is universally acknowledged that, overall, component recording is superior to composite recording.

High-End Digital Formats

The first commercial digital video format was SMPTE D-1 introduced by Sony in 1986. D-1 was a decidedly high-end format featuring component video recording and high-quality audio. However, D-1 was in fact *too* high end, and only a limited number of facilities adopted the expensive format (Schubin, 1993). Two later formats, D-2 (1988) and D-3 (1991), used composite video technology, and thus cost less than D-1. Both formats are used in broadcast and post-production situations (Chan, 1994).

The year 1992 became something of a watershed in the evolution of digital videotape as three companies introduced new formats. Panasonic's D-5 (the designation "D-4" was skipped because it carries connotations of death in certain parts of the Far East) is a component format based on D-3, and can play back D-3 tapes. Ampex's DCT (Digital Component Technology) is aimed at high-end production applications, and is designed as part of a system that includes a proprietary switcher, editor, and DVE unit (Chan, 1994). Sony's Digital Betacam, which also will play back analog Betacam and Betacam SP tapes, is designed to move users of its analog Betacam systems into a digital format. In 1996, Sony introduced the Betacam SX format as part of what it calls a "digital solution for news gathering." The system includes both tape and hard disk storage systems, but is not fully

compatible with either Betacam SP or Digital Betacam (Caranicas, 1996).
Table 7.2 shows a summary of professional digital videotape formats.

Table 7.2
Professional Digital Tape Formats

Format	Intro	Mfgrs	Tape Width	Signal	Sampling Rate	Applications
D-1	1986	Sony	19 mm	Component/ No compression	4:2:2	High-end production
D-2	1988	Ampex Hitachi Sony	19 mm	Composite/ No compression	Composite	High end production, broadcast, industrial
D-3	1991	JVC Panasonic	1/2 inch	Composite/ No compression	Composite	High end production, broadcast, industrial
D-5	1992	Panasonic	1/2 inch	Component/ No compression	4:2:2	High-end production, broadcast, post-production
D-6	1993	BTS	1/2 inch	Component/ No compression	4:2:2	Post-production, image archiving
DCT	1992	Ampex	19mm	Component/ No compression	4:2:2	High-end production
Digital Betacam	1992	Sony	1/2 inch	Component/ Compressed	4:2:2	High-end production, broadcast, EFP/ENG, industrial
Betacam SX	1996	Sony	1/2 inch	Component/ Compressed	4:2:2	EFP

Source: James C. Foust

Recent Developments—Low-Cost Digital

While digital videotape recording made great strides in its first decade, the
technology was at first largely the province of high-end production. Digital
video found its way into large production houses, broadcast outlets, and the

industrial sector, but, until recently, mid- and low-end markets had been passed over by the digital revolution. That is changing, however, as new formats are promising to bring digital technology within reach of many more people.

The push to bring lower-cost digital videotape technology to market is proceeding on two fronts. Manufacturers would like to tap the growing "prosumer" market, filled with both amateur and professional enthusiasts who use video as either a hobby or in small-scale businesses. Manufacturers expect this market to eagerly embrace the increased quality and capability of digital formats as they are made more affordable. The speed and portability also make the formats attractive in electronic news gathering (ENG), industrial, and in-house applications.

Several companies also would like to bring digital video into the home, tapping the vast market of consumers who use their VCRs to record and view television programming and movies. It is estimated that there are currently half a billion VHS VCRs in use, and electronics vendors would like nothing better than to replace these machines with digital systems (Cole, 1995).

Manufacturers have been developing consumer digital tape formats since the early 1980s, but, early on, they did not publicize the work because they did not want to discourage people from purchasing analog formats (Next Video Recorder, 1993). Now, however, with home VCR penetration around 90%, the industry is ready to move consumers to something new (Casey, 1995). To that end, 50 manufacturers have agreed on a new consumer standard called DVC (Digital VideoCassette), sometimes shortened to DV. DVC will use 1/4-inch tape in two cassette sizes: a DAT-sized cartridge that will be used in camcorders to record up to one hour of video and a unit slightly larger than a standard audiotape that will record up to four-and-a-half hours of video (Digital videocassettes, 1995). DVC also will record and play back high-definition television (HDTV) signals, but it will not be backward compatible with VHS tapes. The price—at least initially—will be steep for a home unit, at around $2,000. The first consumer DVC units—in the form of camcorders—were released in 1996. Ultra-compact consumer models from Sony and JVC weigh only about one pound (including battery and tape) and cost around $2,500. By comparison, the three-chip prosumer Sony camcorder sells for about $4,000.

DVC's debut will not mean the end of VHS's evolution—at least not for JVC, the company that originally developed the dominant home format. JVC, itself a member of the DVC consortium, is touting its own digital format, D-VHS (the "D" stands for "data," not "digital"), that will also play back and record standard VHS tapes. D-VHS's initial target market is owners of digital satellite system (DSS) units, who could use the machine to time-shift digital programming. Since D-VHS can only record and play back a digital bitstream, it requires a set-top converter to output to a television. D-VHS will record up to seven hours of digital video on a VHS-sized cassette, and can record other types of digital information such as computer data (Cole, 1995). The company expects to release D-VHS machines in the United States sometime in 1997 at a cost of about $300 more than conventional VHS units.

JVC would also like to extend VHS's influence in the professional market. The company introduced another variant of the format, Digital-S, at NAB's 1995 convention. Digital-S uses VHS-sized cassettes and is backward compatible with standard VHS. The Digital-S line includes a player ($10,500) and a recorder with pre-read capability for dissolves ($19,500). The format records compressed component signals, and a two-machine editing system can perform dissolves and other digital effects that normally require three machines (Smith, 1995) (For more information on editing systems, see Chapter 9.)

Making an even bigger splash at the 1995 NAB, however, was Panasonic's DVCPRO system. DVCPRO is based on the DVC consumer standard and is semi-compatible with it; DVC tapes will play in DVCPRO machines, but DVC machines will not play DVCPRO tapes. DVCPRO uses the same tapes as DVC, but will record only about half as much time as DVC. Thus, the larger DVC tape that holds four to five hours in DVC format will only hold two hours of video with DVCPRO. Panasonic also introduced a medium-sized DVCPRO cassette that will hold one hour of video (Pro Version, 1995).

The format's smaller tape provides at least one advantage over JVC's Digital-S, as Panasonic showed a complete laptop editing system—a player, recorder, controller, and two monitors all in one small unit—that will allow users to edit in the field. The company also is offering an editing VCR ($11,000), an ENG camcorder ($16,900), and other products. SMPTE has granted the DVCPRO system the D-7 designation in order to facilitate industry standardization, and several other companies have announced that they will support the format (Beacham, 1996). Despite its small size and big price tag, DVCPRO's picture quality is comparable to more expensive analog component formats such as Betacam SP (Livingston, 1995).

In 1996, Sony introduced DVCAM, a low-cost digital format that also is based on DVC. However, DVCAM is not compatible with DVCPRO. Sony is targeting DVCAM at business and industrial clients, recommending its Betacam SX system for broadcast and ENG applications (Silbergleid, 1996). Both DVCPRO and DVCAM formats offer integration with disk-based storage and computer networks. Table 7.3 shows a summary of consumer and prosumer digital video formats.

Table 7.3
Consumer/Prosumer Digital Videotape Formats

Format	Tape Width	Cassette Size/ Record Time	Sampling Rate	VHS?	Applications
D-VHS	1/2 inch	Standard VHS; 5 to 7 hours	N/A[1]	Yes	DSS recording; computer data storage
DVC	1/4 inch	S:2.6 × 1.9 inches; 1 hour. L: 4.9 × 3 inches; 4-1/2 hours	4:1:1	No	Consumer VCR format
DVCPRO (D-7)	1/4 inch	M: 3.8 × 2.5 inches; 1 hour. L: 4.9 × 3 inches; 2 hours	4:1:1	No	Prosumer, EFP/ENG
DVCAM	1/4inch	S: 2.6 × 1.9 inches; 40 min. L: 4.9 × 3 inches; 3 hours	4:1:1	No	Industrial
Digital-S	1/2 inch	Standard VHS; 105 minutes	4:2:2	Yes	Prosumer, EFP/ENG

Source: James C. Foust

[1] Since the D-VHS recorder merely records a digital bitstream, it does no analog-to-digital conversion. Thus, it has no sampling rate.

Factors to Watch

In the face of video servers, high-capacity hard disks, and optical storage media, the future of videotape remains bright. Certainly the number of manufacturers working on new formats should be an indication that tape is far from dead. The present situation, however, in which several formats compete for broad and niche markets, presents a dilemma for the professional user. There are so many formats—many of which are similar in terms of quality, price, and features—that deciding which one to use can be a difficult process. While it is reasonably clear that committing to tape is not a mistake in today's changing market, it is often much less clear which tape format best suits individual needs.

With all the rush to develop digital formats, the fact is that analog formats are still the most prevalent in the industry. This dominance is likely to continue for a few years, but, as pieces of analog equipment reach the end of their useful lives in industry settings, it is likely they will be replaced with digital hardware. For now, digital formats have helped drive down the costs of such analog workhorses as U-Matic and S-VHS, making it tempting for start-up and low-budget organizations to invest in analog technology and ride out its declining years.

Some companies are trying to pull users into digital formats by providing backward compatibility with analog formats. This is a good idea for Sony and JVC, which have large installed bases of analog machines. Thus, Sony's Digital Betacam and Betacam SX offer ways for Betacam and Betacam SP users to move to digital without losing compatibility with their existing hardware and tapes, while JVC hopes users of S-VHS will embrace its D-VHS and Digital-S formats for the same reasons.

DVC, at least from the standpoint of the number of manufacturers supporting it, seems most likely to bring digital videotape into the home. Still, its initial price will scare off all but the most ardent videophiles, and its incompatibility with VHS will make many reluctant to adopt it. The fact is that VHS's quality is good enough for most television viewers, and that opinion is not likely to change in the near future. As Johnson (1995, p. H-21) wrote, "The millions of people who sit down each evening to a rented VHS tape have made it pretty clear that convenience and cheapness compensate for a mediocre product."

In the professional market, the future is certainly digital, but the format is uncertain. Television organizations needing to replace equipment face a choice of several formats, and it is unclear which ones will succeed. "There's a lot of risk involved," Fox's Senior Vice President Andrew Setos recently remarked. "There's no safe thing to do" (McConnell, 1995, p. 57). As companies continue to produce new formats, that feeling of risk is likely to grow. As we pass the 40th anniversary of the VR-1000, its legacy is a market bustling with confidence, yet bristling with uncertainty.

Bibliography

Beacham, F. (1996, March 22). Panasonic, Sony unleash rival DVCs. *TV Technology*, 1.

Caranicas, P. (1996, April 12). The "F" word; Video formats. *SHOOT*, 2.

Casey, P. (1995, April). Tape is on a roll. *AV Video*, 83-92.

Chan, C. (1994, January). Studio videotape recorders. *Broadcast Engineering*, 56-60.

Cole, G. (1995, April 21). Addicts delight. *Times Educational Supplement*, p. 22.

Digital videocassettes. (1995, June). *Electronics Now*, 6.

Inglis, A. F. (1990). *Behind the tube: A history of broadcasting technology and business*. Boston: Focal Press.

Inglis, A. F. (1993). *Video engineering*. New York: McGraw-Hill.

Johnson, L. P. (1995, August 20). Videotape's best years may lie in future. *New York Times*, H-21.

Livingston, P. (1995, October). Applied technology: Panasonic DVCPRO. *Broadcast Engineering*, 92-95.

McConnell, C. (1994, March 28). VTRs: Not dead yet. *Broadcasting & Cable*, 38.

McConnell, C. (1995, April 17). The risky business of choosing a format. *Broadcasting & Cable*, 57-58.

Next video recorder—Tape or disk? (1993, February 22). *TV Digest*, 9.

Noll, A. M. (1988). *Television technology: Fundamentals and future prospects*. Norwood, MA: Artech House.

Paulson, B. (1996, October 24). 4:2:2 digital video components: It's here! *Back Stage*, 4B.

Pro version of DVC recorder in 4th quarter. (1995, March 20). *Television Digest*, 11.

Rubin, M. (1991). *Non-linear: A guide to electronic film and video editing*. Gainesville, FL: Triad Publishing Company.

Schubin, M. (1993, March). Format follows function. *Videography*, 27-32.

Silbergleid, M. (1995, February). Industry dabbles with disk-based storage as analog tape perseveres. *Television Broadcast*, 1.

Silbergleid, M. (1996, March). Sony introduces pro DVCAM format. *Television Broadcast*, 1.

Smith, C. (1995, June). A stroll through the NAB jungle. *AV Video*, 49-52, 73.

Van Tassel, J. (1996). Digital video compression. In Grant, A. E. (Ed.). *Communication technology update* (5th ed.). Boston: Focal Press.

Watkinson, J. (1992). *The D-3 digital video recorder*. Oxford: Focal Press.

8

Video Servers

*Steve Jackson and
Jeffrey S.Wilkinson*

Since the development of videotape, the video industry has been searching for the perfect video storage and transmission technology. This perfect technology would be inexpensive and reliable, allow instantaneous access to any video clip in storage, would be portable, and would be easily stored or maintained when not in use.

Unfortunately, no such technology exists. What may be the next best thing, however, *is* available. The convergence of telecommunications and computer technology has led to the development of the *video server*. This device is a computer hard disk that can record and play video and audio over a network. These servers are used in three ways:

• To play back video material on-air, such as commercials or even full-length video programming.

• As the backbone of a true "video-on-demand" (VOD) network. VOD allows cable subscribers to order movies at any time from a file of available movies. With true VOD, the subscriber can control the movie just like it was being played from a home videotape recorder—stopping, watching scenes over again, and skipping over unwanted material.

• As a central video storage facility for production facilities to allow random access of video to several video editing suites, as well as tape duplication of finished products. Video clips are handled just like work files in a business office with a file server. Individual users can manipulate video files, view them, send them to other workstations, or save them to the main server.

Video servers have a number of advantages over older videotape technology. They are non-linear, which means that time is not wasted rewinding a tape to look for a single piece of material. It allows rapid random access to material in any order needed. It can also be cheaper to operate than tape-based systems where video clips must be played repeatedly, saving wear-and-tear on expensive broadcast quality video recorders.

Developers of video servers must consider three factors in order to maximize this technology:

(1)   *Capacity*—Digital video takes up huge amounts of space. An hour of 525-line digital component video needs 76 gigabytes (GB) of space. The old reliable floppy drive, in its current incarnation, can hold only 1.4 megabytes (MB). That means that it takes 54,286 floppies to hold a one-hour segment of video. (Remember that a byte is 8 bits.) Modems are rated in Kilobits per second (Kb/s). That means that a modem rated at 28.8 Kb/s transmits data at around 3,600 bytes per second, or one megabyte every 3 minutes and 40 seconds (Bridges, 1997).

Figure 8.1
Video Servers

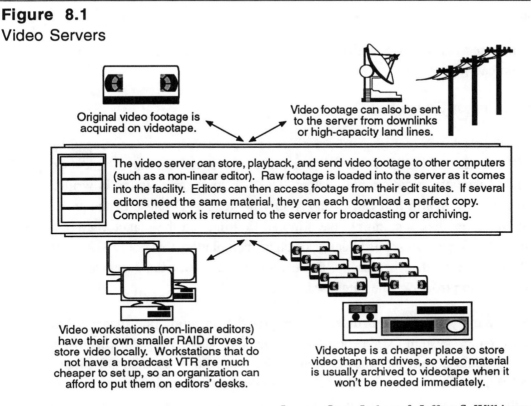

Original video footage is acquired on videotape.

Video footage can also be sent to the server from downlinks or high-capacity land lines.

The video server can store, playback, and send video footage to other computers (such as a non-linear editor). Raw footage is loaded into the server as it comes into the facility. Editors can then access footage from their edit suites. If several editors need the same material, they can each download a perfect copy. Completed work is returned to the server for broadcasting or archiving.

Video workstations (non-linear editors) have their own smaller RAID droves to store video locally. Workstations that do not have a broadcast VTR are much cheaper to set up, so an organization can afford to put them on editors' desks.

Videotape is a cheaper place to store video than hard drives, so video material is usually archived to videotape when it won't be needed immediately.

Source: Steve Jackson & Jeffrey S. Wilkinson

(2) *Speed*—Just because 54,286 floppies could hold an hour of video, it doesn't mean that they could play it in real time. Each second, 21 MB of video information (four channels of stereo audio would require another MB per second at CD quality) needs to be found and sent on its way to the end user. It takes an average computer about one minute to read a full floppy, which means that your hour of video would be able to reach you in about 15 hours (assuming there were a couple of floppy disks with that much storage space).

(3) *Bandwidth*—Assuming a technology can move data at more than 21 MB per second, we then have to think about the channel through which we are transmitting. The amount of data that a channel can transmit at any one time is known as "bandwidth." A 28.8 Kb/s modem can handle around 29,000 bits every second. A megabyte is a million bytes, or 8 million bits, so it would take one hour and 36 minutes to send one minute of video.

Background

Video servers are the result of convergence from three major areas of communications.

Mass Storage for Computers

Hard disk drives (called just hard disks or hard drives) were developed by IBM in the late 1950s. A hard disk is made of material similar to videotape and backed by a rigid circular platter. The disk spins rapidly, and is written and read by an arm that carries the read/write heads. Because of the speed at which the disk is spinning, the arm can find data on the platter very rapidly. Early disk drives used gangs of eight-inch platters that could hold less than 5 MB of data per unit. These units were most often used to store information from on-line databases.

By the early 1980s, hard disks had migrated from corporate management information system (MIS) rooms onto consumer desktops. An early disk drive could access any information on its platter in less than 30 microseconds and hold up to 30 MB of data. At the same time, the first electronic still-stores were being installed in high-end video facilities. These devices used large, very fast (and very expensive) hard drives to store individual video stills. By the late 1980s, large fast-disk arrays were developed that could record video and play it back at broadcast quality. Units such as Abekas's Digital Disk Recorder could record up to 60 seconds of video, but they were very expensive to operate. Users tended to be limited to post-production and graphics facilities.

Networking

Networking is the process of linking two or more computers together. Early networking designs passed several MBs of data per second between dozens of machines. These networks have become known as LANs (local area networks) because the machines must be physically close—housed in the same room, floor, or building, for example. By the mid-1980s, Ethernet LANs were becoming standard in the computing industry, with the ability to pass 10 MB per second over the network. These networks could never pass video data around in real time, however. Uncompressed D1 video, now considered the standard for "broadcast quality," needs a minimum of 21 MB per second.

Compression

Video technology has always been concerned with getting more signal into less space. The NTSC color standard was developed to fit a broadcast color video signal into the space formerly used by a black-and-white signal. In the digital domain, compression has been used for years by the computer industry to trade processor power for storage capacity. Compressed computer files became common with the rise of the Internet and its modest bandwidth. Even with compression, however, copper phone lines and ISDN will probably never be able to carry any but the lowest-quality digital video signal.

Recent Developments

You can tell when a technology comes of age; it is reduced to an acronym. Video servers are possible because of developments in all three of the above-mentioned limiting factors. Each development, furthermore, has its own acronym.

Redundant Array of Inexpensive Disks

RAID is an example of how affordable random access disk storage has become. Large, fast disk drives are very expensive, especially if they are designed to handle video. RAID drives are gangs of inexpensive drives that were developed during the 1980s as a way of linking multiple disk drives to quickly store and retrieve large video files. RAID drives can be configured to either access data very quickly, or to act as a redundant backup system. This assures that data is not lost in case of drive failure.

RAID level 0 is called "striping." This is where the server is configured so that data is spread out across several drives. This allows fast access to data. RAID level 1 is called disk mirroring, where each drive records the same information. While this slightly increases how fast the drives can deliver information, it is primarily designed to assure that if you lose one drive, the data is saved on another. The video industry has now moved to RAID 3, which is a system where data is striped across several drives, but "parity" information is also recorded to another dedicated parity drive. If a drive is lost, the parity drive can be used to replace lost data, which increases reliability. A small number of manufacturers make most hard drives: Quantum, Micropolis, IBM, and Seagate are the biggest players.

Asynchronous Transfer Mode

ATM is a method of moving large amounts of information across a network. ATM divides information into blocks that can be carried by almost any high-speed network. ATM is not a networking technology, but a system that makes networking technology transparent to the video signal, allowing the data to move through a data network in real time.

In most computer networks, data being sent from one computer to another enter a pipeline with all of the other data on the network, and move on to the destination. A computer network is an excellent way to move data that is not time-based (such as e-mail). This system can cause problems with video. A busy network will take bandwidth from a user to cover its increased demands, which results in slower transmission of information. For a video editor downloading a video segment, this would not be much of a problem unless the network became overloaded. On the other hand, if you are trying to send real-time video somewhere, a delay or loss of data will result in lost video frames.

ATM, instead, creates a circuit from the server to its destination, and holds that circuit as long as data is being sent. This assures there will be enough bandwidth available to transmit the video without delay (Hassay, 1996). Another advantage of ATM is that it is being widely adopted by the telephone industry.

Moving Pictures Expert Group

MPEG is a system of compressing video information. MPEG-1 was the first standard developed primarily to allow CD-ROMs to carry video. MPEG-2 is a newer standard that allows multiple resolution and compression rates, and may become the industry standard. The advantage of compression is that it saves disk space and allows larger files to be transmitted over limited bandwidth systems. MPEG-2 is called a "lossy system" which means that it discards some information from the video picture, but the losses are almost imperceptible except at high compression rates.

The amount of compression applied to a video signal is called its compression rate. A 21 MB per second signal with a 2:1 compression rate needs 10.5 MB of storage space for each second. MPEG compression has been adopted by the DBS industry, but a different version was chosen for the Digital television standards supported by the Advanced Television Systems Committee (Van Tassel, 1996).

Current Status

Video servers are becoming standard in three areas of electronic media: news production, commercial insertion, and video-on-demand systems. In news production, video servers act as a central repository for the most current video information. Videographers in the field shoot tape, then return to the station and download their taped material into the video server. There, it can be edited or viewed by anyone with a computer editor hooked into the video system. This means, for example, that at 5:00 P.M., a station can roll live video from a breaking story and, at the same time, an editor can be pulling segments from the same video for a package to be aired at 6:00 P.M. Archival news footage is also being placed on server systems for quick access by all non-linear editors within a station or network.

Figure 8.2
Video Servers for News Production

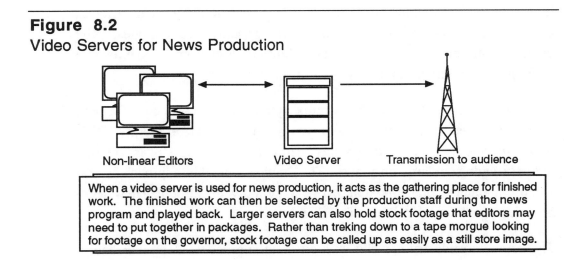

Non-linear Editors   Video Server   Transmission to audience

When a video server is used for news production, it acts as the gathering place for finished work. The finished work can then be selected by the production staff during the news program and played back. Larger servers can also hold stock footage that editors may need to put together in packages. Rather than treking down to a tape morgue looking for footage on the governor, stock footage can be called up as easily as a still store image.

Source: Steve Jackson & Jeffrey S. Wilkinson

Broadcast and cable stations have also begun to put their commercial insertion onto video servers. Previously, most stations used a rack of high-quality videotape players attached to a tape library. These robotic systems, such as the Sony Betacart, are very reliable, but they are also expensive and require a large amount of human labor to load and unload tapes from the bins. In addition, these robotic systems were not easily expandable; adding a second channel to a facility often meant buying a second spot insertion system. According to Steve Rowell (assistant chief engineer at WOFL-TV in Orlando, Florida), their video server saves time and money by enabling them to easily program a second channel out of their station. This ability to program multiple channels without the expense of an additional tape-based system is one of the driving factors behind video server installation (Dickson, 1996).

Video servers using RAID technology can hold several hours of commercial spots. Commercials in the RAID drives are "on-line" and ready to go. Many servers can handle insertion on several channels simultaneously, saving the cost and complication of having to keep large numbers of duplicate videotapes on hand. In both cases, videos not in the lineup are stored off-line on videotape.

Factors to Watch

Video servers represent the convergence and the clash of two technological industries. The computer industry and the video industry have different approaches and philosophies regarding their respective technologies. The video industry has always demanded reliability in its equipment. Unreliable equipment will only be adopted if there is no other alternative.

Compatibility is another factor. A properly maintained U-Matic VTR built in 1985 (or even 1975!) can still be a part of a modern video facility. This is because the broadcast industry has been relatively successful in creating industry-wide standards on video. The drawback to this approach is that video equipment companies tend to be very slow to introduce new technologies into the market at an affordable cost.

The computer industry has chosen a different approach. Computer equipment tends to be developed and upgraded very rapidly, often without time taken for the bugs to be worked out in either the software or the hardware. As a result, computer equipment is often seen as unreliable. With the present rate of innovation, equipment is rapidly surpassed by new equipment, and the older equipment is typically left unsupported. The computer industry has also had a difficult time defining standards, with DOS, Macintosh, and UNIX carving out niches in the marketplace.

This clash in industry philosophies has delayed the introduction of computers into the mainstream video production environment. It has also meant that the market for video servers is in flux. Although Hewlett-Packard, Tektronix, and Quantel are three well-known manufacturers making video servers, dozens of other firms are currently in the market. With the rapid changes inherent in the video server industry, however, it is difficult to tell which manufacturers will still be in the server business in the future.

Most video facilities will incorporate video servers in the near future. One survey reports that 57% of all broadcast television stations plan to move toward video server technology by 1999, added to the 19% that already had servers installed in their facilities in 1996 (Silberglied, 1996).

Despite this movement to video servers, tape is far from dead. The current trend is for acquisition and archiving to be done on digital tape, with material in current use being kept either on a central video server or on local arrays of hard drives. Some traditional manufacturers of video equipment have recognized this and begun to develop hybrid digital videotape recorders (VTRs) that incorporate hard drives, and use the same MPEG compression that the servers use. The first of these hybrids, Sony's Betacam SX, uses commonly-available (and relatively cheap) analog Betacam SP tapes and includes a hard drive.

Integration of this equipment will allow facilities to add video servers into those areas of their production and broadcast operations where they save money and offer real benefits to the operators, without having to go "totally tapeless," as impressive as that term would seem. An example of a hybrid system was operated by NBC during the 1996 Atlanta Olympics. NBC used Tektronix Profile "disk-based storage devices" with a capacity for four-and-a-half hours of Betacam SP quality video. Most of the work in the tape room was done with digital videotape recorders, but the "Profiles" segments allowed highlight reels to be built even as video was being recorded by the traditional VTRs (Hallinger, 1996).

If a faster Internet connection becomes widely available to individual households at a low enough cost, video servers will also make their appearance with Internet providers and programmers. Here, they operate just like a regular file server. They store information and send it to users when it is requested, just as when they hit an HTML tag on their World Wide Web browser. Instead of downloading a single picture or a short low-quality video file, they would be able to send full-screen, live video to a home computer.

One service that is further away is true video on demand. The cost of hard drive storage is lower than ever before (around $0.40 a megabyte for RAID arrays), but it is still too expensive to justify the storage and computing overhead associated with VOD (Smith, 1996).

Although hard drives will continue to drop in price, they may have competition. Digital versatile discs (DVDs) will be on the market by mid-1997. DVD is a high-capacity, read-only compact disk technology—a CD-ROM on steroids if you will—that will hold more than 5 GB of data (a two-sided disk will hold almost 18 GB). The huge capacity of these disks, along with their ability to play back broadcast-quality video, will offer consumers a way of watching an interactive, high-quality video program right from their own homes. While some distance off, this technology could be used in place of some of the functions of video servers. While the disks are not currently rewriteable, a commercial or movie could be "burned" onto a DVD and then played back from an inexpensive player. Disks should be fairly inexpensive and have a long shelf life.

Good video servers are on the market now, but getting the industry to move away from tape remains a challenge. Broadcast VTRs sell themselves on their price and performance. They are reliable and easy to use. In technical manuals for VTRs, there are detailed maintenance schedules with specific points at which parts must be replaced (after 500 hours, 1,000 hours, etc.). For video servers, one manufacturer claims that its disks have an average "mean time between failure" of 500,000 hours—or 57 years of constant use! Although hard disks have become very reliable, it remains to be seen whether they have become *that* reliable.

Broadcasters must accept the notion that computers are not as reliable as the tape transports they have replaced. Broadcasters cannot ignore the fact, however, that computers are less expensive to operate. This means a station can afford to have some spares available. That is part of the idea behind RAID drives—redundancy increases both speed *and* reliability.

The computer industry should find a way to standardize and produce equipment that doesn't become obsolete with the next update. It is important to note that obsolescence is something that the consumer side of the computer industry has been fighting for years.

If and when the Internet moves into wider bandwidths, video programmers may find that video servers are the only way programming can be delivered. These video servers will simply be bigger versions of the Internet servers in use today. Again, reliability and ease-of-use will be the key.

In the meantime, video servers allow facilities to change the way they work. Large video projects can now be edited by teams of people, all with access to the same video material. This means that ambitious projects can be turned around much faster than with tape-based systems. Video editors, paintbox and 3-D artists, audio editors, and scriptwriters can all work on projects at the same time, sending files back and forth across the production center's network.

Another area not yet tapped is education. Teaching video production techniques takes a new twist when a communication department installs a video server. Professors can leave unedited video on the server for student use. When the students finish a project, they can file it onto the server, where the professor can easily evaluate it. Not only will this help professional education, but it will allow students from other disciplines to learn video production techniques.

Video servers, along with non-linear editors and paint boxes, represent the tools of the computer era finally making their way into mainstream production. Some areas of video production—notably video acquisition—will remain tape-based. But random access disk-based systems will be the primary way that studios will do business. The industry is ready to spend money on these systems, but many engineers (who are the ones that install and maintain the systems) are waiting for the technology to prove itself. At the rate this industry is moving, they will not have long to wait.

Bibliography

Bernier, P. (1995, 27 November). When HDTV meets asynchronous transfer mode. *Inter@ctive Week.* [On-line]. Available: http://www.zdnet.com/intweek/print/951127/bandw/doc4.html.

Bridges, J. (1997). *An Internet guide for mass communications students.* Madison, WI: Brown and Benchmark.

Cooper, L. F. (1996 August). Are you ready for ATM? *Byte,* 85-90.

Dickson, G. (1996, December 2). Systems integrators ride strong market. *Broadcasting & Cable,* 64-66

Hallinger, M. (1996, September 27). Tape rooms touch disk future. *TV Technology,* 6 (Olympic Supplement).

Hassay, J. A. (1996). Broadband network technologies. In A. E. Grant (Ed.). *Communication technology update* (5th ed.). Boston: Focal Press.

Silbergleid, M. (1996). Digital leads the way: Tape and disk high on buy list. *Television Broadcast, 19,* 1, 86.

Smith, B. (1996, August 19). Stations eagerly await digital video on demand. *Broadcasting & Cable,* 44-50.

Van Tassel, J. (1996). Digital video compression. In A. E. Grant (Ed.). *Communication technology update* (5th ed.). Boston: Focal Press.

Zettl, H. (1997). *Television production handbook* (6th ed.). Belmont CA: Wadsworth.

9

Linear Editing Systems

Sheila E. Schroeder

In the world of video and audio editing technology, a key factor never changes: Users have always demanded a cost-effective system that is compatible with existing formats so that archived material is not irretrievable. As the media environment changes, however, other factors become increasingly important: New products need to incorporate digital technology, and they must be flexible and offer field and studio-based editing options.

An examination of most innovations in linear video editing technology over the last several decades reveals two stories. One is a tale of format integration as various manufacturers developed products based on technology standards like VHS, 3/4-inch U-matic, and, more recently, S-VHS. Suppliers attempted to appeal to various markets with their own product lines of cameras, VCRs, time base correctors, graphic interfaces, editing systems, and the like. A competing narrative developed as manufacturers attempted to set industry standards and keep innovations "within the company," as is illustrated by Sony Betacam and Panasonic MII formats.

As different compression standards are adopted for digital technology, old issues continue to surface about designing technology within an Open Media Framework (OMF) in which different manufacturers "are emphasizing the need for integrated production and operations components linked by high-speed computer networks" (Dickson, 1996b, p. 63). Present-day technological introductions are no exception as the largest manufacturers of linear editing equipment—JVC, Panasonic and Sony—have each introduced digital linear editing products for prosumer, corporate/industrial, and high-end television broadcasting and production house markets. Sony has promoted a "total systems concept," while Panasonic, Tektronix, Silicon Graphics, Hewlett-Packard, Avid, and over 25 other companies support the "open systems" philosophy for digital broadcast equipment (Livingston, 1996; Giardina, 1996).

This chapter explores contemporary developments in linear editing systems which, contrary to rumors of their impending demise, are still widely used by TV news operations, post-production houses, and in corporate and educational settings for various off-line and on-line applications. Along with highlighting technological innovations which continue as we move from analog to digital technology, this chapter will take an issues-based approach to clarify why particular innovations are being made and how these innovations will influence content, for what one sees on television is the result of both editorial and technological decisions.

Background—Analog and Digital Signals

Analog video editing continues to be an industry standard, but recent trends in the telecommunications field indicate that analog systems will eventually be replaced by their digital counterparts. The primary difference between these two technologies is in the recording of the video signal. According to Zettl (1992), "[a]nalog systems record the continually fluctuating video signal as created and processed by a video source (such as a camera) on videotape and retrieve the recorded information as an identical *continually fluctuating* signal from the videotape" (emphasis added) (p. 289).

Digital systems use various forms of sampling to record analog images and sounds. The analog signal is converted into binary numbers which are assigned to the amplitude and frequency characteristics of the analog signal. A major advantage of digital recording is that the binary numbers "are largely immune to signal interference, system noise, and general distortion" (Whittaker, 1993, p. 23). In theory, this means that there is insignificant loss after multiple generations of digital duplication or editing.

Foremost among the factors precipitating the change from analog to digital recording are:

- Digital technology offers superior video and audio quality.

- Digital tape formats are more portable.

- Digital signals may be transmitted over telephone lines, thus diminishing the need for cumbersome and costly satellite trucks.

- Digitized signals can be processed by a computer.

- Digital equipment features a negligible loss of quality in the editing and duplication process (Mirabito & Morgenstern, 1990).

A brief look at the changes in analog editing technology illustrates the predictable patterns manufacturers have historically followed and which, in part, continue to drive the transformation to digital technology. For example, new editing systems have addressed on-going industry concerns about quality, cost, portability, and the manufacturers' goal of continually developing new products for users. In educational institutions where budgets continue to undergo scrutiny, replacing efficient, cost-effective systems like the affordable JVC Edit-Desk package seems like exceptionally long-range planning. Digital retooling in educational settings will, no doubt, follow the lead of industry as schools supply the next generation of creative and technological personnel. The editing environment for students, however, will continue to demand flexibility and adaptability as they are called upon to produce creative ideas with ever-changing technology.

Advantages of Digital Linear Editing

- Edited digital signals are virtually immune to quality loss.

- Digital tape is smaller (6.35mm wide) and more portable than previous formats.

- Digital signals can be transmitted over telephone lines.

- Digital signals can be processed by desktop computers and do not rely on devoted, single-function editing systems.

- Digital signals have better sound and visual quality than analog signals.

- A/B roll editing requires only two decks when using digital editing technology.

Recent Developments—Digital Linear Video Editing

A review of videotape formats can be found in Chapter 6, but, for purposes of this chapter, some duplication is necessary. Videotape editing technology has been shrinking from one-inch systems that require a roomful of editing gear to half-inch and quarter-inch rack mounted (and the new portable) systems that compete with one-inch quality and reduce user costs substantially. Betacam SP and the less popular MII are examples of these smaller format professional systems. The move from three-quarter-inch U-matic tape to half-inch S-VHS and quarter-inch Hi8 illustrates the continuing shift in technological options for various product users, from high-end broadcast applications to prosumer operations.

New editing equipment invariably accompanies tape format changes. Most of the edit system innovations over the last decade have provided users with digital transitions, effects, and graphic layering options. The basics of editing systems and their operation have not changed significantly: One or more decks feed a switching unit which outputs the signal onto a master record deck. Now, however, digital technology is changing the entire editing process.

Figure 9.1

Elements and Information Flow in Linear and
Digital Desktop Video Systems

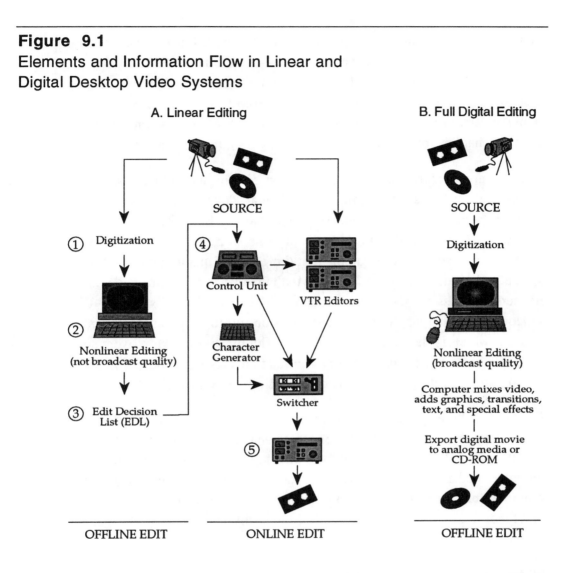

A. Linear Editing   B. Full Digital Editing

Source: Y. M. Rivas & J. A. Meister

Digital linear editing systems provide what appears to be a transitional tape-based format as various manufacturers seek to develop disk-based acquisition systems that some predict will eventually bypass tape altogether. In the meantime, according to Panasonic's Phil Livingston, disk technology is best suited for random access for post-production and release, while video-tape has many practical benefits including high-quality, cost-effective acquisition and archiving (Livingston, 1996). Manufacturers of digital linear editing equipment are counting on the relatively low cost of digital tape and its backward compatibility with existing formats to create a market for the new generation of linear editing systems (McConnell, 1996). In addition to the cost effectiveness of tape-based storage—McConnell (1994) reports that digital tape stores video for about $0.05 per megabyte, while the cost for disk storage is estimated at approximately $0.60 per megabyte—there are many advantages to digital video technology. Some of these are discussed in other chapters, but a few are worth highlighting in this context.

Recent improvements have concentrated on picture and sound quality and on portability. The DVC (digital video) format, developed by a consortium of manufacturers, is a linear video format used in both the prosumer and professional markets that touts a signal-to-noise ratio two to three times better than existing VHS equipment and offers CD quality audio—all on a specially designed metal evaporated (ME) tape that is 6.35 mm wide and is housed in a cassette shell that is roughly 1/12th the size of standard VHS videocassettes. A single digital tape can store up to 11 gigabytes of information, which is the equivalent of 7,500 floppy disks. Moreover, some cassettes have an optional memory chip that enables fast random access to video clips after downloading to a hard disk system (Anzicek, 1995).

Creating multiple generations of tapes during post-production has always been a primary concern for editing professionals. Reduced picture degradation is a compelling selling point for digital tape technology. With digitally-recorded media, not only is the initial video and sound recording better than previous analog recordings, but a principal advantage of digital recording is that the first generation is nearly indistinguishable from subsequent generations.

Still early in product development, the newest digital linear editing systems seem to be marketed to specific end users, especially electronic news gathering (ENG) entities, as the larger news organizations move toward a one-person "crew" called a video journalist who shoots, reports, edits, and distributes news packages. News agencies require speed and efficiency in gathering footage, in producing packages, and in disseminating the information. Digital technology aids in all aspects of news production, and all of the major manufacturers have designed competitive ENG/EFP high-end DVC systems with these clients in mind.

Panasonic developed DVCPRO, while Sony competes for this non-consumer market with DVCAM. JVC has also developed Digital-S, a half-inch tape that is backward compatible with S-VHS. Interestingly, Panasonic engineers have figured out a way to play Sony's DVCAM metal evaporated tapes in Panasonic machines by adjusting the servo speed to compensate for track pitch differences (Dickson, 1996c). This may alleviate concern among users over format incompatibility between these two manufacturing giants.

To answer the need for speed in news package production, all three have developed two-deck A/B roll editing systems. Digital technology in the form of built-in hard drives permits the elimination of the third deck by using pre-read editing which facilitates multi-generational layering and A/B roll editing with only two VTRs. To perform dissolves and other effects, the systems store the clips from which transitions are desired on the hard drive. Citing portability, ease-of-use, and a short learning curve for its video journalists, Time Warner's 24-hour all-news regional cable service *New York 1* decided to purchase over $1 million worth of DVCPRO equipment for their operation (Jessell, 1996).

Panasonic has developed a single-unit laptop Field Edit Package, while Sony's DVCAMs most efficient use is with its desktop non-linear Edit-Station. Sony's DVCAM uses ClipLink memory technology in their tapes that enables videographers to mark scenes as "OK" or "NG" in camera on-the-fly. This facilitates the editing process by pre-marking the "good" clips, allowing editors to go directly to the desired material. Furthermore, the ClipLink Log Data records up to 198 index pictures, small thumbnail video images that identify each take. They are stored at the end of the recorded tape and form a visual reference for GUI (graphical user interface) computer-based editing.

JVC offers a pre-read editing system operable with either digital or analog signals so editing with S-VHS and Digital-S can be accomplished within the same system. Pre-read technology has only previously been available through costly high-end digital systems. Despite being a member of the DVC consortium, JVC sees a need for "a digital format that is downward compatible to the existing S-VHS" (Anzicek, 1995, p. 17). JVC has designed Digital-S as a bridge technology to cement the link between the large installed base of S-VHS editing systems with its new half-inch digital format, much as Sony has done with Digital Betacam. Fox News Channel will use Digital-S for feed recording, editing, and playback in its all-digital studio in New York and in its Washington bureau (Dickson, 1996d).

Meanwhile, Fox SportsNet intends to use Digital-S for all sports news and all pregame highlight editing (Dickson, 1996e). These are strong endorsements of a format that is positioned to fill a niche in educational institutions because of its compatibility with VHS.

Another production concern linked with timely editing has been the ability to transfer video and sound from tape to computer disk. All the major DVC manufacturers have developed systems that accomplish this task at four times the regular, real-time speed. One primary drawback to using linear tape formats (either analog or digital) with non-linear editing systems has been the necessity to download (and digitize analog footage) field material in real time. The ability to accomplish this at 4× speed will be a significant feature for deadline-based operations such as television news. (This function is discussed further in Chapter 10.)

Factors to Watch

Because digital systems are more stable and require less maintenance than comparable analog configurations, the motivation to convert to digital has become even more enticing (Mirabito & Morgenstern, 1990). And, as with most new technologies, the start-up costs will continue to decrease as formats are adopted and refined. For instance, current costs for prosumer DVC technology are under $4,000 for a high-quality, three-chip camcorder such as Sony's DCR-VX1000.

Manufacturers are courting some of the emergent news organizations such as Fox and Video News International (VNI) which have adopted Digital-S and Panasonic DVC and DVCPRO, respectively (Dickson, 1995; 1996a). Other organizations, such as Cox Broadcasting, have opted for "total digital solutions" by having Sony design, supply, and integrate its new digital facility for WSB-TV in Atlanta (Dickson, 1996a). According to Sony, one of the important advantages of adopting their system is that each piece is designed with the others in mind; thus, they all share the same compression scheme. This eliminates artifacts caused by decompressing and recompressing video signals (Giardina, 1996).

Nevertheless, as further innovations in this groundbreaking technology develop, it seems predictable that editing will move away from linear systems toward non-linear environments. In fact, Avid and Ikegami have teamed to produce CamCutter, the first camera that uses a digital recording unit to transfer video directly to a hard disk for desktop editing. This eliminates the time lost to digitization and digital transfer. However, costs for each 20-minute hard-drive cartridge, about $2,500, make this an expensive format. Both companies, however, have also endorsed DVCPRO as a format for digital news gathering (Jessell, 1996).

It is predictable that, whatever changes take place, compatibility with existing in-house formats will dictate future purchases. For instance, facilities that use Betacam and Betacam SP will likely look to Digital Betacam as they convert production and post-production facilities to a digital format. Likewise, most S-VHS users are likely to adopt Digital-S because of its backward compatibility with S-VHS.

It is difficult to predict what the effects of digital linear editing will be on various production environments. Since many educational institutions instruct students with low-cost, non-linear, computer-based editing options such as Adobe Premiere and do not have the same need for speed as news agencies, look for them to possibly skip major purchases of digital linear editing gear. On the other hand, if hybrid digital tape/disk systems become widely adopted in the years to come, educational institutions may adopt DVC technologies as system acquisition costs drop (Mazor, 1995).

With an enormous base of analog linear systems and hundreds of thousands of hours of archived tape in television stations, the most important market will be in news departments. Specifically, journalists who are shooting, writing, and editing packages as part of one-person reporting crews in 24-hour-a-day news operations are well-suited to take advantage of the benefits of digital systems. This trend has important consequences as newcomers will need to acquire a broad range of storytelling, shooting, and editing skills to operate in tomorrow's video production environment. While production technology will decrease in size while increasing in performance, the ability to conceptualize and communicate creative ideas in both written and verbal formats will be timeless attributes that will serve producers well into the 21st century.

Bibliography

Anzicek, M. (1995, October). The new digital tape formats: Can yesterday's tape be a solution for tomorrow's needs? *Tape-Disc Business,* 17.

Dickson, G. (1995, December 11). VNI picks digital video cameras. *Broadcasting & Cable,* 91.

Dickson, G. (1996a, April 17). Sony makes $13 million digital deal with Cox. Will provide end-to-end solution at WSB-TV Atlanta. *Broadcasting & Cable,* 14.

Dickson, G. (1996b, April 22). Systems are the solutions at NAB. *Broadcasting & Cable,* 63.

Dickson, G. (1996c, May 27). Panasonic finds bridge over DVC divide. *Broadcasting & Cable,* 48.

Dickson, G. (1996d, August 26). Fox News Channel chooses Digital-S. *Broadcasting & Cable,* 55.

Dickson, G. (1996e, September 9). Fox SportsNet goes Digital-S. *Broadcasting & Cable,* 59.

Giardina, C. (1996, March 15). Sony's stand: Solutions, solutions, solutions. *Shoot,* 7.

Jessell, H. A. (1996, April 17). DVCPRO tape format on a roll. *Broadcasting & Cable,* 14.

Livingston, P. (1996, June). Trends in image recording: The case for digital video recording—On tape, now. *Advanced Imaging,* 16.

Mazor, B. (1995, May). NAB '95: Front end to back, historic for imaging pros. *Advanced Imaging,* 34.

McConnell, C. (1994, March 28). VTRs: Not dead yet. *Broadcasting & Cable,* 38.

McConnell, C. (1996, March 4). Camera makers focus on digital at NAB. *Broadcasting & Cable,* 55.

Mirabito, M. M., & Morgenstern, B. L. (1990). *The new communications technologies.* Boston: Focal Press.

Rivas, Y. M., & Meister, J. A. (1995). Desktop video production. In A. E. Grant (Ed.). *Communication technology update* (4th ed.). Boston: Focal Press.

Whittaker, R. (1993). *Television production.* Mountain View, CA: Mayfield Publishing Company.

Zettl, H. (1992). *Television production handbook* (5th ed.). Belmont, CA: Wadsworth.

10

Non-Linear Video Editing

Ron Osgood

While attending a national video conference several years ago, a respected video producer made the statement "we don't need linear anything anymore." I was not ready to accept this statement at the time, but I am convinced that it is true today. An in-depth look at the current state of digital video in television news operations and video post-production facilities will readily confirm this.

The digital video signal revolutionizes how television programs are produced. Now, the computer can replace many expensive pieces of specialized hardware. As one writer who covers the video industry says, "...a revolution is about to begin in new media. Hollywood had better be prepared as newcomers produce quality video equal to that of the major studios" (Braitman, 1996, p. 39). One competitor in sales states "the computer is fast becoming an integral part of professional post production. Every day more video studios rely on the flexibility of digital technology to complete successful productions with lowered costs" (Fast Video Machine brochure, 1996).

Background

In order to process video through a computer, it must be digital. Until a few years ago, many in the television industry thought of digital video as signals recorded on digital videotape, which were then edited using traditional linear techniques in the post-production process. Those in the computer industry compare the storage and processing of time-based (motion) data on computer media (hard drives, etc.) with the same basic techniques by which text and still images are manipulated. The merging of these two views is probably a more accurate description.

Currently, the vast majority of video is acquired on analog videotape. This linear format has been in use for more than 40 years. These first-generation tapes are edited on traditional linear video editing systems. However, as anyone who has ever edited videotape knows, the limitations of a linear system are readily apparent. It can be time-consuming, frustrating, and expensive to make changes to a completed video program. Analog videotape also suffers a loss in quality with each subsequent generation. Digital technology has a clear advantage since there is almost no quality loss when copying a digital signal. Ideally, the copy is an exact clone of the original file. Another benefit of the digital signal is that it allows producers to use non-linear video editing as an alternative post-production tool.

With non-linear video editing, random access to any point in the timeline is simple. This means that changes to any element, regardless of time or length, can easily be made after the program has been completed. To understand this, think of how the computer and word processor transformed the process of typing. With a typewriter, changes in the typed page were difficult—if not impossible—once the page was completely typed. Word processing software allows simple cutting and pasting any time a change needs to be made—even after a document has been completely finished. With this same process of cutting and pasting, changes can easily be made to the audio and video files that make up a digital video program.

Once the actual work session begins, the capabilities of the non-linear process are apparent. The ease of dragging clips and creating effects and transitions varies from system to system, but the basic premise is that you can try a technique, change it, or eliminate it with a simple keyboard or mouse command. While most effects, including a simple dissolve, might take longer to actually complete in a low-end non-linear system than with a multi-source videotape editor because of computer rendering time, it is much easier to change duration, trim the edit points, or move the transition with a non-linear system.

Photo courtesy of VideoSphere

Rendering is the final stage in the computer process where all elements are blended together. Most high-end systems have enough memory and speed to process the effects in real time. Adding filters (such as converting a scene from color to black-and-white), adding lighting effects, distorting the image, and many others are simple tasks with a non-linear editor. Digital audio capabilities usually add four or more channels of audio with the capability of mixing, equalizing, panning, fading, and adding filter effects. Many non-linear systems include some titling and graphics capabilities. Although some are simple and limited in scope, others have the power of an expensive stand-alone graphics computer.

Figure 10.1
Non-Linear Editing Process

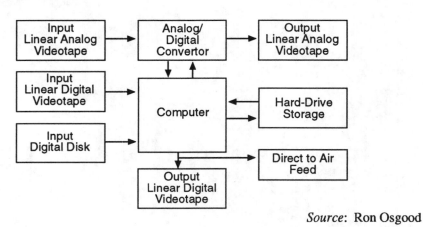

Source: Ron Osgood

As mentioned earlier, one of the major benefits of a non-linear system is the ability to change specific elements within a program without starting over. Avid, for example, offers 32 levels of undo with their software (Avid MCXpress brochure, 1996). This feature alone can make the life of an editor easier. With such technical freedom, the editor is free to spend time creating and recreating the program without the worry of losing a completed segment.

Since non-linear editing can only work with a digital signal, analog video-tape must be transferred to digital form through a process called digitization. Digitization converts the signal from analog to digital storage (hard drives in most cases). This is a real-time procedure; that is, a 10-minute clip will take 10 minutes to digitize.

It is also possible to record the video on digital linear tape. These video clips are already in digital form and can be transferred to disk in a process similar to copying computer files. This process is quicker than the real-time transfer required for digitization. The Sony DVCAM uses a high-speed link which allows data to be transferred at four times the speed and creates a clone of the original (Sony EditStation brochure, 1996). A third possibility involves a camera system which uses a digital disk recorder instead of tape. Once acquired, an edit decision list can be organized, and initial decisions on which clips to use can be accomplished right in the camera. This can save time for the ENG team that is driving back to the station to begin editing. Once at the station, the disk can be loaded directly to the non-linear edit system through a device called MediaDock (Ikegami DNG brochure, 1995).

As advantageous as non-linear seems, there are some drawbacks. If the producer is working with analog tape as the original medium, the process of digitizing is time-consuming. While this forces the editor to review and log footage for optimum results, some projects might take longer to complete using non-linear editing than using traditional linear editing techniques. For example, many news editors can have a news package edited on tape and ready for air while their non-linear counterpart is still editing.

Another drawback is the massive amount of storage required for video files. One solution is the use of compression to help make more efficient use of limited storage space. Compression is the encoding of a file with a special algorithm to reduce space requirements for storage (Multimedia Demystified, 1994). The speed at which the computer processor can throughput (pass) the files is critical. Any time compression is used, the chance for a loss in quality or the introduction of digital artifacts is increased.

Recent Developments

Until recently, customers of digital video editing systems were almost always found at high-end agencies creating broadcast TV ads and music videos. Short segments that require plenty of fast cuts and special effects are still the best fit for these non-linear systems, but with maturing technology, lower prices, and cheaper multigigabyte, video-friendly storage, non-linear editing is spreading to the larger world of video editing professionals (Barron, 1996).

Added reliability and lower cost are the most significant recent developments in non-linear video. Manufacturers have offered updated software and improvements in hardware that have helped clear up the technical problems evident in some of the previous versions of their products. Stiff competition in this industry has kept costs under control and, in some cases, decreased system prices.

A feature many manufacturers are offering is real-time effects. This feature alone will make the process more appealing to those who found the rendering time of an effect to be a disincentive to switch to non-linear editing. While some systems include the ability to perform dissolves, wipes, and other effects with a basic system, others are optional. Both Avid's Media Composer Xpress and Media 100 offer two options: One includes a feature called fast rendering, and another allows real-time effects. For those with larger budgets, Scitex Digital Video's impressive line of Sphere systems include real-time effects.

Many systems support a standard that allows sharing between software programs. With this feature, add-on software modules with effects, graphics, and filters can be utilized. Fast's Video Machine is an example of a system that allows a variety of drawing, compositing, and graphics files to be integrated into the program.

An impressive audio feature of the Media 100 is eight tracks of CD-quality audio that mix in real time. This feature, combined with balanced audio connectors and the ability to adjust the audio level during playback, make this an extremely valuable component of the system.

The flexibility of a hybrid system can be a serious option for those who have a difficult time justifying the purchase of a system which might make existing equipment obsolete. The hybrid system allows linear tape and non-linear digital sources to be edited into the same program. Sony's Edit-Station allows use of up to four VCRs in conjunction with the non-linear source. Sony also includes a feature called Disk B-Roll which allows a disk copy of a tape to become an additional source for match-frame editing (Sony EditStation brochure, 1996).

Photo courtesy of Avid

With non-linear video, an effective producer can enter the post-production phase with the knowledge that some mistakes can easily be fixed, and that the time spent making changes and fine-tuning the program can be shortened considerably. Likewise, it is an editor's dream to be able to create multiple versions of a completed project to share with a client. Many of the problems that producers have dealt with through the linear tape era have vanished as a result of the non-linear process. "In the past, people have had to scrap programs...when things changed. If you've got an EDL, you can just redigitize the material, insert a new technique or procedure, and extend the life of the program" (Bawarsky, 1996).

As with many computer software programs, the computer (screen) interface varies from manufacturer to manufacturer. Some are more intuitive to members of the video community, others make more sense to those from the computer industry, and still others are more intuitive to film editors. The convergence of the three industries has forced users to learn new technologies and techniques. For example, most video editors would probably have laughed at the term "print to tape" several years ago. Now, it has become as common as "dubbing." One might find it comical when a video professional talks about 30 frames to a computer professional who responds "you mean 60 fields" while discussing one second of broadcast video.

Table 10.1
Selected Sample of Non-Linear Systems

Product	Manufacturer	Price	Features
Premiere	Adobe	Low	B, I, J
MCXpress	Avid	Medium	C, E, F, H, I
Media Composer 8000	Avid	High	C, D, F, I
Media 100	Media 100	Medium	C, E, H, I
VideoSphere	Scitex	High	C, D, H, I
EditStation ES-7	Sony	Medium	C, D, J

Key

A	Hardware only	F	JPEG
B	Software only	G	MPEG
C	Hardware & software	H	M-JPEG
D	Real-time effects	I	Macintosh
E	Real-time effects option	J	Windows

Price (*less* computer)

Low	Under $1,000
Medium	$10,000-$25,000
High	Above $25,000

Source: Ron Osgood

The actual screen interface is another potential source for intuitively different styles. Adobe's non-linear video editing software program Premiere has an interface that displays a timeline with an A and B video channel (Adobe Premiere user's guide, 1994). This visual style reminds traditional video editors of the A/B-roll tape editing process. Panasonic's Postbox uses one video timeline to display all video clips in the sequence (Panasonic Postbox brochure, 1996). Without an interface or terminology standard, you can imagine the potential confusion which exists when looking at different systems.

Factors To Watch

The trend toward improved quality at lower prices in non-linear editing systems will continue in the near future. As manufacturers continue to provide faster processing and larger storage capabilities, the efficiency of using the computer for digital video production will continue to increase. Third-party software plug-ins and compatible software will be available as system options in the future. In addition, the use of digital linear tape and, eventually, digital disk recording will expand as costs decline. The advent of video servers and distribution technologies which handle video materials will have a positive effect on how producers work in the future. It won't be long until editors access video materials using methods that were only dreams in the recent past.

"Those systems that stay native throughout the process are the ones which will thrive. We shouldn't need the worry of going from analog to digital and back, with compression schemes throughout" (Mark Abeln, personal communication, December 15, 1996). Regardless of what new techniques and hardware become available, the systems in use today will continue to meet the needs of video producers in the near future. These systems are the ones that can be updated, will allow added capabilities, and are efficient to work with. We must not forget that, although the tools of the trade always change and improve, our goal is to communicate through effective visual storytelling.

Bibliography

Adobe. (1994). Adobe Premiere user's guide.

Avid MCXpress. (1996). Product brochure.

Barron, D. (1996). *Video professionals flock to digital editing.* Hyperstand. [On-line]. Available: http://www.hyperstand.com/.

Bawarsky, D. (1996). *Video professionals flock to digital editing.* Hyperstand. [On-line]. Available: http://www.hyperstand.com/.

Braitman, S. (1996). *Trinity World, 39.*

Fast Video Machine. (1996). Product brochure.

Holsinger, E. (1993). *MacWeek guide to desktop video.* Emeryville, CA: Ziff-Davis Press.

Holsinger, E. (1994). *How multimedia works*. Emeryville, CA: Ziff-Davis Press.

Ikegami DNG. (1995). Product brochure.

Media 100 Digital Video System. (1996). Product brochure.

Multimedia demystified. (1994). New York: Random House/New Media Series.

Ohanian, T. (1993). *Digital non-linear editing*. Boston: Focal Press.

Panasonic Postbox. (1996). Product brochure.

Play Incorporated. (1996). Product brochure.

Radius. (1996). Product brochure.

Scitex Digital Media. (1996). Product brochure.

Soderberg, A., & Hudson, T. (1995). *Desktop video studio*. New York: Random House.

Sony EditStation. (1996). Product brochure.

Turner, B. (1996, August). An editor's view of NAB '96. *Videography*, 66-88.

11

Video Production Switchers, Special Effects Generators, and Digital Video Effects

Suzanne Williams

The video switcher is the very heart of the television control room. Until recently, it was primarily a routing device utilized to combine separate images into a video stream. However, with the advent of digital technology, both the function and the architecture of the switcher have changed dramatically. The video manipulation capabilities afforded by digital technology, when added to the analog switcher or incorporated into the digital switcher, have transformed modern switchers into multi-purpose production tools.

In the process, there has been a paradigm shift in the technology associated with the switcher. As video manipulation functions have become more complex, upgrading analog switchers has only been possible through new, more complex hardware or by adding digital video effects (DVE) equipment to existing systems. Upgrading digital technology is far less costly and cumbersome since the major design elements of digital systems are in the software. Therefore, changing an existing system requires merely the installation of new software or cards with the necessary memory expansion to process the upgrade. In addition, digital technology is much more flexible than analog. Each button on the analog system is dedicated to a relay, and reconfiguring the system requires changing the hardware. With digital switchers, each function can be attached to nested menus which increase the versatility of each interface, or the switcher itself can be reconfigured by changing the operating program. Finally, the price of digital technology is falling dramatically, and Amiga-based systems are bringing to live production video manipulation capabilities once only afforded by high-end, post-production houses.

Background

The earliest designers of television production studios and control rooms envisioned the necessity for a video switcher—to combine video from a variety of sources into a visual output. Hutchinson (1946) reports that, during the experimental period of 1930s, "almost all the switching was done by fading one camera out and, when the screen was empty...fading the other camera in" (p. 33). While in black, a button activated a crosspoint switch that changed the video source fed into the outgoing line (Morris & Shelby, 1937). By the time regular television transmission began in the mid-1940s, switchers could instantaneously change from one video source to another, called "snap switching" at that time or "cutting" now (Hutchinson, 1946). The name "switcher" evolved from the fact that video transitioning devices then, and until recently, were mostly crosspoint switches. This is in contrast to European video mixers which were more like audio mixers with slide faders for each source (Birkmaier, 1990).

Many of the early improvements to the switcher involved the transitions from one video source to another. A second bus and a fader bar was added to the switcher, and a second transition—then called a "lap dissolve," now simply "dissolve"—was possible. With this transition also came the first video effect—the superimposition—created when the dissolve was stopped midway between two sources. By 1946, the next improvement to the switcher was already on the horizon—special effects generators or oscillators which output a variety of geometrically-shaped waveforms and produced patterned transitions between sources called wipes (Krupnick, 1990). When a wipe was stopped midway between two sources, a second video effect was possible—the split screen.

As television's first decade of regular operation was coming to a close, a third video effect was added to the switcher that began to significantly alter the video. The luminance key allowed one picture to be electronically cut into another, with the cut being determined by the luminance—the light or dark portions of the keyed image. With the development of color television, the chroma key was added where the cut for the key was determined by a color, and color generators, which produced a variety of background colors, became standard. For the second and third decades of television, these transitions—the cut, dissolve, and wipe—and special effects involving superimpositions, split screens, and keys formed the basis of all production switchers. Refinements to wipes included horizontal and vertical multipliers that allowed for the creation of hundreds of wipe patterns, and generators that altered wipes and split screens by the inclusion of a border between the two images, the ability to make the edge of the border hard or soft, the insertion of a background color into the border, and the alteration of the symmetry of the border. A "joy stick" was also added in order to reposition the starting point of the wipe or the split screen effect.

During the first decade of television, the architecture of the switcher was dictated by the requirements for live, real-time programming or programming that was to be recorded without editing. However, there were two major forces which changed the course of the development of the switcher—the invention of videotape recording systems in the mid-1950s and the introduction of digital technology in the mid-1970s.

The ability to edit video made it feasible to develop complex special effects in the editing booth. Thus, the switching requirements of live programming and edited programming began to diverge. Live programming required easy access to a wide variety of inputs and the ability to quickly set up any necessary special effects. Post-production situations required fewer readily-available inputs and allowed the time to develop very complex special effects. In order to bring many of the effects that could be generated in the editing booth (such as multi-layered keys and split screen effects involving more than two sources) into live broadcasts, additional mix effects capabilities were added to existing switchers. "Double re-entry" capability meant that the effect, whether it be the split screen or key, was routed into a second mix effect bus to form the basis of other changes in the image.

The development of the video image as it moves through a switcher is typically compared to a stream. Upstream effect buses are those which are located first within the main switcher architecture, while a downstream effect bus is one which occurs later as the video is developed (although the term "downstream" often refers to the final mix-effect buses in the stream after the image leaves the switcher's main architecture). Early analog switchers used a cascading re-entry system in which the mix-effect subsystems were linearly or serially arranged, i.e., the output of one mix-effect subsystem was input into any of the mix-effect subsystems that occurred after it (or downstream) in the switcher (Krupnick, 1990).

The Central Dynamics, Ltd. (CDL) 480 series switcher was the first system to use the multi-level effects architecture including re-entry systems. However, a major problem with early systems was that the operator was forced to identify and prioritize the layers of the picture and then arrange them according to the switcher's architecture to get the desired image. Much greater control over the design of the image was provided by the introduction of the Grass Valley Group's 300 series switcher. The 300 gave the operator the ability to change layer priorities in the mix-effect bus and to re-enter effects into upstream as well as downstream mix-effect buses (Birkmaier, 1990). Thus, the switcher became more complex as additional mix-effect buses were added upstream and downstream.

By the mid-1970s, the computer began to have a significant impact upon both live and post-production switchers, but in different ways. The development of character generators added computerized graphic attachments which could easily be keyed into live and edited programs. However, the early importance of the computer for the switcher in live production situations lay in the control it afforded in creating complex special effects. Microprocessers were coupled with analog systems, as in Grass Valley's E-MEM effects memory system for its 1600 series video switchers. The microprocessor allowed the advanced set-up and recall of very sophisticated, multi-level programmed effects, which were often too time-consuming for a fast-paced live program such as a newscast. This system was described as being "elegant but very hardware intensive" (Birkmaier, 1990, p. 97). It was DVE technology that resulted in the most dramatic change in the function of the switcher and of its physical makeup. Although transitioning between sources was still a necessary feature of the switcher, the excitement over digital technology was in the impressive new flexibility in video manipulation that it provided.

While analog switchers had to be content with wipes in which the video did not change in size or configuration as it was being replaced on the screen by another image, digitization allowed the size and shape of the video image to easily be altered. Therefore, images could be slowly compressed in size until they disappeared from the screen, rolled into a ball and spun off the screen, etc. Also, on the analog switcher, wipes were limited to geometric configurations, while digital technology provided the capability to develop intricate wipes using a variety of shapes. It also enabled the creation of unique wipes such as those used currently on the situation comedy *Home Improvement.*

With analog technology, few changes in the image can be effected through keying or patterned segmentation of the screen, but with DVE technology, the image can be compressed and repeated, creating an echo effect. Using analog systems, the over-the-shoulder graphic inserts used in conjunction with news anchors began as either rear screen projections or monitors mounted in the set; later, images were carefully framed in the upper right-hand corner of the screen to facilitate a split screen or key effect. The advent of digital technology allowed the image size and shape to be altered, and live images could be compressed and placed in the boxes in any portion of the screen. Also, the image could be stretched either horizontally or vertically or distorted in perspective so that it looked three-dimensional.

With paint systems, portions of the image may be changed or removed, or the entire image may be altered for special emphasis. Such alterations include:

- A mosaic effect in which the image is broken down into squares (to simulate mosaic tiles).

- Posterization in which the variation in color shades is reduced, resulting in less color detail and a picture that looks as if it was painted with a limited pallet.

- Solarization in which the variation in brightness is reduced, resulting in minimal shading thus producing a high-contrast image.

- Texturization in which a variety of textures may be mapped onto images.

In addition, frame store units allow the operator to capture and store still images to be replayed upon command.

Early digital equipment tended to be so expensive that only sophisticated post-production houses could afford it. One of the first digital switchers was the Abekas A84, which could handle 12 separate inputs and could generate eight layers of keying, each of which had a full key processor with independent masking capability and color correction. Another was the Grass Valley Kadenza, which could handle five layers, any of which could be Kaleidoscope digital effects channels. However, the cost of each of these switchers was originally over a quarter of a million dollars (Birkmaier, 1990; Johns, 1988). It was not necessary to have a digital switcher in order to benefit from digital effects. Add-on, dedicated digital video effect generators became the most common means of achieving sophisticated digital effects; however, even entry-level systems were costly in the late 1980s. In 1992, Ampex offered its ADO 500 which included high-quality 3-D page turns for approximately $60,000, a price that was described as being 65% of the cost of comparable effects packages (Lambert, 1992).

The entrance of computers into the video production arena created a paradigm shift in terms of the hardware. Analog systems in the late 1980s were described as being elegant, but hardware intensive. With computerized technology, the elegance and design features were in the software, while the hardware provided the operating mechanism. Upgrades to the system were no longer hardware dependent; they could often be made very easily by changing the software. Thus, in 1992, the marketing strategy for high-end Dynatech Colorgraphics systems was to urge entry level through the DP/Paint which included graphics, rotoscoping, and matte (approximately

$60,000), and then upgrade as needs changed to DP/Animator (which included all of the above features plus 2-D and 3-D animation) or DP/MAX (which offered real-time layering and color correction). Further, the life of dedicated hardware could be expanded through software and memory upgrades. For example, in 1992, Abekas introduced a 10-bit DVE machine but, at the same time, to owners of its Abekas A72 Digital Character Generator, it offered free software along with additional memory to enhance the shading, light source, and animation capabilities. This gave it effects associated with high-end paint systems (Lambert, 1992).

Even with declining costs and efficient upgrades, the technology remained so expensive and time-consuming to operate that it was impractical for most live productions and was mostly found in post-production suites. However, in 1990, a young company, NewTek, that had only been in business for five years changed the face of the video production industry. For the first time, complicated effects that had been the domain of very expensive systems in post-production houses were brought into the budget range of most producers. NewTek introduced the Video Toaster 1.0, a programmable card housed in a Commodore Amiga 2000 or 2500 computer (a computer originally designed for video games and, therefore, designed to manipulate and display video). The Toaster was designed to provide the features of six dedicated machines at one-tenth of their combined cost. It included:

(1)   A traditional switcher interface with a color background generator and luminance keyer.

(2)   A digital effects module with a broad array of specialized wipes.

(3)   A dual channel, 24-bit framestore and framegrabber.

(4)   ToasterCG, a full-feature character generator program.

(5)   ToasterPaint, a 24-bit paint program.

(6)   Lightwave 3D, a three-dimensional modeler/renderer/animator.

Although all of these functions could be found in separate devices and in high-end editing equipment costing $60,000 or more, the cost for the Toaster was extremely low by professional standards—$1,595 for the circuit boards and $1,599 for an Amiga 2000 or $3,799 for an Amiga 2500. The Toaster was not a game or a toy. but worked with incoming synchronized signals to create "an affordable professional video production tool" (Yager, 1991, p. 245). Although one of the major criticisms was that when the video was downsized the image became blocky and aliased (Desktop Video Market, 1995; Yager, 1991), it was felt that some of the other features could produce the look of high-end systems—with user-friendly ease (Atkin, 1993). A series of Video Toasters were daisy-chained to create animation segments for the television series *Babylon 5* using the bundled Lightwave 3D software, a very sophisticated system considering its low acquisition cost.

Recent Developments

The impact of the Toaster was not only to make impressive digital effects affordable, but it also changed production technology by integrating a number of stand-alone devices into one piece of equipment. In the editing suite, it provided switching, character generation, and video manipulation capabilities, and, when coupled with an external switcher, it was a low-cost digital effects and character generator. In order to compete with the Toaster, DVE companies were forced to offer similar features.

One of the few to offer them all was Pinnacle Systems, a relatively new company founded in 1986. Pinnacle Systems was already an established top producer of DVEs when it introduced Alladin in 1994. Alladin is an integrated system with a four-input, component digital switcher, and it includes luminance and chroma keying as well as a full set of digital transitions with the ability to customize wipes through its AlladinPaint system and its digital special effects generator. Its DVE system offers such specialized transitions as page turns, water ripples, dynamic highlights and shading, trail and sparkle effects, and positionable drop shadows. The digital effects are clean and anti-aliased (the sharp or ragged edges of fonts and graphics have been electronically smoothed to provide a more polished look) and have been judged to be better than that of the Toaster (Desktop Video Market, 1995). The system includes a frame grabber and still store as well as supporting software including AlladinPaint, a character generator (Image North Inscriber CG), and 3-D animation software (CrystalGraphics' Crystal TOPAS Professional). It also creates customized wipes by capturing a graphic, assigning Alpha levels with AlladinPaint, and using the DVE generator for the wipe (The Pinnacle Alladin, 1995). Allain (1995) notes,

> The ability to input and use an eight-bit linear key signal in
> digital video effects is one of the outstanding features of the
> Alladin. Ampex pioneered this feature—often described by
> traditional DVS [digital video effects] system manufacturers
> as a flying key—with the ADO. Once, with higher-end
> units, a flying key option alone could have cost about the
> same as the entire Alladin system (p. 76).

What makes both the Toaster and now Pinnacle's Alladin stand out from multipurpose systems that include a DVE is that most don't offer 3-D and curvilinear effects, particularly for .$9,990 for the composite version (excluding the recommended 486 DX computer) or $11,480 for the component version.

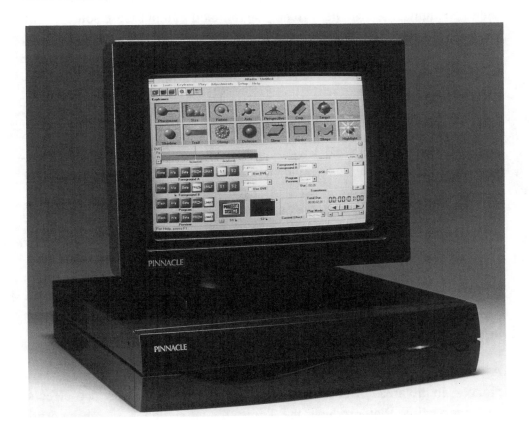

Photo courtesy of Pinnacle Systems, Inc.

In this transitional period between analog and digital control rooms, there are a number of options for the video professional. Although Tektronix's Grass Valley Group still offers several analog switchers, it offers a much wider array of both component and composite digital production switchers, most of which have analog and digital inputs. Recognizing not only that some purchasers may be waiting for digital technology to become more affordable, but also that analog may still be adequate for live production situations, ECHOlab is offering the MVS9, an analog control panel that is digital-ready. When the digital chassis is available, purchasers will have the opportunity to trade in their analog chassis, and they will only be charged for the difference in price between the analog and digital systems.

Digital switchers are also offering greater flexibility in their configurations. Philips BTS Diamond Digital Switchers offer keyers which feature router integration so that one switcher is capable of controlling up to six router buses. Thus, if the production situation calls for two cameras and several videotape units, the switcher can be programmed to input these sources with the proper labeling appearing on the correct input button. If the production calls for four cameras, the switcher can easily be reprogrammed without the time-consuming and costly rewiring required of earlier switchers.

Digital switchers are also incorporating more features that were previously supplied by stand-alone, dedicated equipment. Tektronix division Grass Valley Group, a traditional leader in the switcher field, offers the Model 4000 line—three switchers which include three mix-effect buses, each of which can produce a composited four-layer video or a composited four-layer key. Model 4000 also includes an Effects Send system which allows the operator to feed digital effects devices such as the Grass Valley Krystal 4300 or to splice the Krystal system into any of the keyers in the mix/effects subsystems. It has unlimited mix/effects re-entry and six matte generators in each mix-effects subsystem with a wash capability in every matte generator. In addition, it has a frame grabber, which grabs the key signal in order to easily layer stills.

A new competitor in the field is Play, Inc., which was founded in 1994 by pioneers in the areas of desktop video (such as the Toaster), video effects, and video paint. Play produces the Trinity digital switcher, which incorporates a programmable keying engine, independent color correctors for each input, organic wipe patterns, two still-store channels, and a color background matte generator. Its KeyBrush technology allows the operator to draw freehand linear key channels and garbage mattes in real time. In addition, Trinity allows the overlay of animated graphics on video sources and color space remapping to create diverse effects such as sepia tone, monochrome, day-for-night, solarization, embossing, posterization, etc. on each live input independently and simultaneously. Further, the latest Play digital technology is providing effects in real time that have previously been available only in post-production equipment. For example, Trinity offers the following options:

- The addition of up to eight Warp Engines to its motherboard to facilitate having several warped video streams on screen at once.

- Real-time morphing between 3-D shapes.

- Light sources which cast highlights and shadows on warped video in real time.

- Mapping of live video onto organic shapes such as blobs, liquids, and clouds.

- Personal FX which allows the creation of custom effects.

Play has also included paint, animation, and compositing in one effects technology called Panamation. In this technology, the drawing modes work with a pressure-sensitive airbrush in real time and offer:

- Natural media brushes (watercolors, oil paints, chalk, pastels, and charcoal).

- Natural media surfaces (papers, woods, cloth, and stones).

- Adjustable light sources.

- The ability to animate any stroke with real-world physics.

- The ability to texture map, perspective map, rotate, warp, shear, or shew any brush.

Thus, Trinity is designed to be an all-inclusive production system, incorporating a switcher, DVE, titling, animation, editing, and audio (Fraticelli, 1996).

Table 11.1 provides a comparison in cost and features of a digital switcher designed for real-time broadcast applications (Grass Valley Group 2200), a compact switcher designed for broadcast and/or edit suite applications (Sony BVS-3200C), a digital switcher with digital multi-effects designed primarily for the edit suite with flexible system integration (Sony DFS-500), and a desktop video tool (Pinnacle Alladin 601).

Factors to Watch

Major issues still to be resolved for digital switching and video effects involve platforms and architectures. At the high end, Discreet Logic has been hailed for its development of open system software, such as its compositor Flame that runs on Silicon Graphics workstations. Although Flame is not cheap ($585,000 per system), one does not have to buy the proprietary hardware as with similar Quantel systems (Deck, 1995).

At the low end, the Toaster was designed to run on the Commodore Amiga, and some feel that one of its strengths is the fact that its software has been created specifically for its applications and is not adapted from other existing software. Thus, it has been designed to work within an integrated environment so that files created in one application can easily be incorporated into another (Desktop Video Market, 1995). However, since the Alladin uses a Windows platform, an image, with its key channel, can be sent digitally to the Alladin from a Macintosh workstation. And, Pinnacle Systems' David Hopkins (DVE Business Manager) feels that the future of the industry is in the development of a Mac- or Windows-based common platform. In response, NewTek has released a stand-alone unit for platforms running Windows NT and Windows '95.

Table 11.1
Comparison of Digital Switching
and Effects Technologies

Brand and Model	Inputs	Features	Cost
Grass Valley Group Model 2200 Component Switcher	32 video or key inputs - any mix	2 M/E w/2 keyers per M/E for 7 layers of video in one pass. Memory system with 100 registers; each register supporting effects of up to 50 key frames. Virtually unlimited wipes - 70 pat. w/opt.second gen. (additive or non-add. mix) & size, position, multiplication, & aspect ratio modifiers. Options: Borderline key edge gen.; frame store - video, key and mask; Krystal DVE port; redundant power supply; talley; editor ports.	$118,000 average. Depends on configuration.
Sony BVS - 3200C Component Switcher	8	1 M/E w/2 keyers & downstream keyer for 5 layers of video in one pass. 10 wipe patterns & may assign 8 matrix wipe patterns to 2 user buttons. 10 registers for storage of switcher parameters. Interface for BVE-910/9000 editor, DME-450 Digital Multi Effects, & GPI/talley.	$29,400
Sony DVS - 500 DME Switcher and Digital Multi Effects	4	Title Keyer. Over 300 wipe pat. include page turn, ripple, etc. Effect modifier for mosaic, posterization, etc. & size, density and amplitude. 40 programmable effect registers. 16 preset color background patterns. 100 snapshot memory registers. 5 matte generators. Genlock capability. Optional DSK board and trail, shadow, and lighting board.	$18,400
Pinnacle Alladin 601 Desktop Video Tool	4	Virtually unlimited wipes - assigned pat. may be modified or new pat. created w/ NTSC keyers & DVE. Real-time 3-D DVE sys. (incl. page turns, ripples, etc.). Drop shadows, borders, highlights, trails. Character generator. Paint. Still store (size of reg. depends on hard-drive space). Optional control panel with joy stick, T-bar, and button controls.	$16,490

Sources: Product brochures and interviews[1]

---

[1] Sources include product brochures and interviews with Doug Harrison, Tektronix; Tom Hooper, Pinnacle Systems; and Sony Business Information Center representatives.

In order to move Toaster technology to Windows, NewTek had to create an external unit that contains the Video Toaster Flyer (a non-linear editing system), a simplified Video Toaster, and a Motorola processor to control them. Also, although Windows NT has many of the features of the AmigaDOS, its weakness is in the editing software; thus, real-time transitions are limited to cuts and fades while all other transitions must be rendered. However, Windows opens up a much larger market for the Toaster, so there is already a movement toward a common platform.

Another factor to watch is the new emphasis upon "systems"—"integrated production and operations components linked by high-speed computers"— the focus of NAB '96 (Dickson, 1996, p. 63). The debate centers around how to develop these systems. Sony introduced its "total system concept" in 1995, which seeks to provide all components of the system. Sony is also pushing its DVCAM format, which differs in track pitch and tape stock from Panasonic's DVCPRO, which has been adopted by at least 20 companies (including Philips BTS and Ikegami), as the image acquisition element in their hardware and software systems. The manufacturers which have adopted DVCPRO are calling for an "open systems" philosophy in which components from several suppliers are incorporated into one system.

This open systems philosophy has led to alliances between manufacturers that otherwise might have competed. Tektronix has an agreement with Silicon Graphics which guarantees interoperability between their digital video systems. Tektronix, Silicon Graphics, Hewlett-Packard, Avid, and Panasonic are all supporting the Fibre Channel networking protocol. Tektronix has also developed a systems integration division to support its efforts in this area (Dickson, 1996). Alladin is the central video effects and compositing engine for the editing systems of Avid, Matrox, Fast Electronics, BTS, TAO, United Media, and Videomedia (Pinnacle Systems, 1996). Also, Pinnacle Systems and NewTek are collaborating to market the Pinnacle GeniePlus and NewTek LightWave which produce transitions previously only available with larger post-production systems such as the Quantel Paintbox. Any of the 3-D transitions included in the GeniePlus Genie Wipe (such as page turns, page folds, water ripples, waves, etc.) can be used to transition in real time between a keyed LightWave bitmap and another source, for example, two keyed live video layers.

A final factor to watch is the change in switcher architecture. Just as more and more functions are being engineered into one device, more functions are being included within each interface. In older switchers, each button activated one function. Thus, it is possible to simplify the vast array of switcher buttons, while not compromising the picture-altering capability of the equipment. For example, the Sony BVS-3000 series switcher includes 10 conventional wipe patterns; however, there are two user buttons to which eight matrix wipe patterns may be assigned. This unit is also easily connected with the DME-450, which expands the capability of the switcher to include more than 100 2-D and 3-D effects. One may doubt that this integration will reach Birkmaier's dream of the ultimate one-bus switcher, where "each video input would have the equivalent of a complete mix/effect system to determine the shape of the jigsaw puzzle piece(s) of the picture contributed by that input" (Birkmaier, 1990). The software of digital switchers makes it possible to nest menus or to reconfigure the inputs into each interface, which increases the functional capabilities of each switch and reduces the necessity for a vast array of them. Looking into the distant future, the development of voice recognition technologies may someday make push-button technologies a thing of the past.

Bibliography

Allain, C. (1995, February 1). Alladin's magic. *Videography*, 76, 78, 80, 90, 112.

Ambrose, G. (1996, November 29). Pinnacle works magic at GRA. *TV Technology*, 51.

Atkin, D. (1993, December). Compute choice awards—Video hardware: Video Toaster 4000. *Compute!*, 22.

Birkmaier, C. (1990, March). Mixed priorities. *Videography*, 91-104.

Brophy, K. A. (1992, June 1). Video Toaster 2.0's special effects amaze. *InfoWorld*, 100.

Deck, S. (1995, November 27). Discreet effects. *Computerworld*.

The desktop video market: A battlefield? (1995, July). *Channel 1*. [On-line]. Available: http://www.vfx.com/vs.html.

Dickson, G. (1996 April 22). Systems are the solutions at NAB. *Broadcasting & Cable*, 63-64.

Fraticelli, E. (1996, June). Content manipulation for production. *Broadcast Engineering*, 86-88.

Grass Valley Group Inc. (1993, April). *Designing digital systems*. Grass Valley, CA.

Hutchinson, T. H. (1946). *Here is television: Your window to the world*. New York: Hastings House.

Johns, A. (1988, November). Abekas rolls 601 switcher in U.K. *Millimeter*, 13.

Krupnick, M. A. (1990). *The electric image: Examining basic TV technology*. White Plains, NY: Knowledge Industry Publications.

Lambert, P. (1992, March 23). Graphics: Filling the gap between high and low. *Broadcasting*, 69-70.

Morris, R. M., & Shelby, R. E. (1937). Television studio design. In *Television: Collected addresses and papers on the future of the new art and its recent technical developments*, Volume II. New York: RCA Institutes Technical Press, 178-193.

The Pinnacle Alladin. (1995, July). *Channel 1*. [On-line]. Available: http://www.vfx.com/alladin.html.

Pinnacle Systems. (1996, February 16). *STUDIOPAK adds advanced functions to Pinnacle Alladin*. News Release of Pinnacle Systems.

Schaaf, D. (1991, November). Let them eat toast. *Training—Supplement*, 43-48.

Yager, T. (1991, March). NewTek's Video Toaster makes professional video affordable. *Byte*, 245-254.

12

Lighting Equipment and Techniques

Bill Holshevnikoff

L ighting for television and video production has evolved slowly for most of the past 50 years. Although there have been great leaps in electronics in the television industry, the craft of illuminating subjects and locations for film, television, and video production has remained basically the same throughout the decades. We still use lights to reveal shape, form, texture, and depth, and the basic design of standard lighting instruments has changed very little.

As with many other industries, the electronic equipment used in television production has become smaller, lighter, and more capable. But there are many productions working today that use much of the same lighting equipment that was used 20 to 30 years ago. Many television stations throughout the United States are still using older lighting instruments that were purchased decades ago when the stations first opened. The reason for this longevity in studio lighting equipment is simple—lights have very few moving parts and, apart from lamp replacements, there is little that can go wrong with a lighting fixture that hangs from a studio grid for years.

Consequently, changes in the lighting world are less dramatic than in other areas of production and post-production. Most of the changes that have occurred within the last two years are improvements in design and efficiency, or features have been added to a product that already has its place in the industry. There are also new lighting products and accessories that have made their way to the film and video industry via photographic and concert lighting manufacturers. These inter-industry relationships are becoming more commonplace and benefit lighting professionals in all aspects of lighting for production.

Although immensely important, lighting is only one aspect of the entire production process. There are countless new electronic products that concern the camera and the process of image-making, but, again, the evolution of lighting equipment over the past decades has been slow. Therefore, this chapter will examine the major updates and advances in lighting equipment over the past several years, and will also look at the continued evolution of production style and techniques that affect the process of lighting.

Background

Lighting for television and video production can be broken into two major categories: studio and location lighting. Because of the nature of studio programming, there has not been a great need for change in studio lighting design or equipment. Much of what has changed in studio lighting is due to the addition of remote-controlled instruments from the concert and stage lighting world and the evolution of computer-controlled dimmer boards. As previously mentioned, many lighting instruments that are decades old are still in daily use by studios producing network-level programming. Mole-Richardson, one of the earliest manufacturers of lighting equipment (since 1927), still produces sturdy instruments with the familiar red steel housing that are very similar to instruments produced in the 1950s. These and other instruments of the past were quite heavy, but they were built to withstand the rigors of studio or location work, and consequently, many are still in use today.

What has changed significantly over the past five to 10 years is the world of location production. Recent developments in portable video camera systems, such as Sony's and Ikegami's digital camera systems, have changed the way location productions are created. The primary improvements that have occurred in both the video and film world are in *image resolution* and *light sensitivity*. Film stocks and television cameras of the past required great amounts of light to produce acceptable images. For television cameras, this was due to the less sensitive image pickup tubes (which are nearly obsolete today) and to camera lens design. Lenses of the past produced noticeably better pictures when operating at or near the middle of the f-stop/iris range, which meant that more light was needed to make pictures. Working with these older camera systems demanded that production crews transport large, heavy studio lighting fixtures to all types of locations just to make acceptable pictures for even the smallest production.

The development of the CCD image chip opened the door to creating smaller video cameras that required much less light. Advances in lens design have also allowed cameras to produce excellent imagery with the lens iris wide open, again allowing the image-maker to work with less light. The combination of these factors has led to the idea of taking small production crews all over the globe to produce some fairly complex programming.

With the newer, more light-sensitive cameras, the need for large, heavy studio lighting fixtures on location has changed. Although larger instruments are still used in-studio and on-location (primarily to light larger spaces), smaller, lighter instruments were suddenly all that was needed for many location productions. This has led to a new generation of smaller, more efficient lighting instruments that are now used on all types of film and television productions. The increase in location production has been the driving force in the design of several new lighting technologies and instruments that also have changed the studio lighting environment.

The past 15 years has also seen the use of HMI lighting expand to all segments of the film and video industries. HMI (Hydrargium Medium arc-length Iodide) lights are powerful, daylight color-balanced lights (Ferncase,

1995). The mixture of mercury and iodide gases produce a light output (5,500°K) that matches the color temperature of midday. HMI lights are available as Fresnel-lensed lights and Par lights. Par stands for Parabolic Aluminized Reflector, which is a type of sealed-beam lamp that resembles a round car headlight (Box, 1993). HMI Par lights put out an extremely narrow and intense beam that can be altered by placing different glass lenses in front of the instrument. By doing so, the beam spread can be changed from an intense, narrow beam to a less-intense wide beam. Only the newest generation of HMI Pars allow for some range of spot and flood control (Holshevnikoff, 1995a). The real magic of an HMI light is that the output of a 1,200 watt Par can equal that of approximately 3,500 to 5,000 watts of tungsten light. Also, the light is already corrected to daylight color, *and* the power consumption is just over 10 amps. If you're battling the brightness of the midday sun outside a window or if you just want to generate a lot of daylight-balanced light, these lights can make the work of the director of photography or the video crew much easier.

The need for smaller, lighter instruments for location work has also produced a healthy competition in the manufacturing side of HMI lighting instruments. Companies such as Arriflex, LTM, Mole Richardson, Cinemills, Sachtler, DN Labs, and K5,600 have been hard at work developing lighter, more compact and more efficient HMI fixtures. Once seen only as an instrument used to match the color temperature and intensity of the sun, older HMI lights had a magnetic power ballast that weighed a minimum of 40 pounds—and that was for the smallest 1,200-watt instrument. Using current computer design and technologies, HMIs now are lighter and more efficient and are available in all sizes, from 125 watts to 12,000 watts. As with all good things, HMIs do have a down side—a hefty price tag. The new ArriSun 1,200-watt Plus Par has a list price of approximately $8,500. If your budget or production needs do not warrant this kind of expense, you can rent this light on a per-need basis for a reasonable daily rental price of $135 to $175, depending upon your market.

The television industry has also seen the proliferation of fluorescent lighting technologies. It was a specific need for location lighting on a film shoot almost 15 years ago that led to the development of the product named Kino Flo, and now many other fluorescent systems have followed (Holshevnikoff, 1995b). Conventional fluorescent lighting fixtures consistently posed a problem for film and video shooters. There are some very nice qualities about fluorescent lights, such as their soft light quality, quick light drop off, low heat, and low power draw. But the problems of poor color rendering (often causing a sickly greenish cast in skin tones), noise, flickering, and large, bulky fixtures outweighed the benefits. Consequently, the concept of using fluorescents on location has been only a tease for most shooters.

Fluorescent fixtures for studio lighting have become standard in many studios. Companies such as Videssence, Kino Flo, Strand Lighting, Light-Tech, and Balcar have produced controllable fluorescent fixtures that are used now on news and interview sets around the world. The big advantage to using fluorescents in the studio environment is that, over a period of time, the low power draw and low heat output can save a studio thousands of dollars in air-conditioning bills. KCRA-TV in Sacramento, California was one of the first television stations in the United States to convert to fluorescent studio lighting in 1989 (a Videssence system), and they were able to reduce their air-conditioning load by 85%. Lamp replacement is also only a fraction of the cost of a standard tungsten lamp. Also, on-camera talent like the look and feel of the soft, cool light. Still, there had not been an acceptable, color-corrected fluorescent fixture suitable for location work.

Kino Flo fluorescent light fixtures were developed primarily for location film and video work. The fixtures are extremely lightweight and durable, and are available in a variety of fixture sizes and lamp configurations. Kino Flo offers 2,900°K (warm tungsten balance), 3,200°K (tungsten balance), and 5,500°K (daylight balance) fluorescent tubes. The double-ended tubes are full-spectrum in color, and they are engineered to respond to the way that video and film stocks collect light. Used as a key or fill source, the new fluorescent instruments are a vast improvement over the use of traditional cool white fluorescent tubes with a color-correction gel, such as Great American Markets GAM Tubes, slipped over the tubes.

Fluorescent lighting fixtures are available in a variety of configurations. The four-lamp, 48-inch Kino Flo fixtures are becoming a popular choice for location production. The company compares the output of this fixture to that of a 1,200-watt HMI Par bounced off a piece of foamcore. The advantages of using fluorescents over the HMI setup are lower power consumption (only 3.5 amps for a four-lamp fixture) and the need for less set space. Tube lengths of 24" and 15" are also available with Kino Flos. Videssence and many other fluorescent manufacturers utilize single-ended tubes for most of their studio instruments, but double-ended tubes are also used for some studio and location instruments.

On the opposite end of the size spectrum, there are little 9" fluorescent instruments which are ideal for car interiors and product work, and tiny, pencil-like wand lights that can be used for accents on sets of all types.

Some fluorescent systems for use on location are designed with a remote ballast that powers the fixtures, much like an HMI light, while most studio fixtures are designed with a built-in ballast. Kino Flos, Videssence, and other fluorescent fixtures are currently being used on the sets of motion pictures, television series, and commercials, and they are now finding their way into the corporate and industrial video world as well.

One other major change in film and video lighting has been the transformation of the photographic softbox to work with the larger and much hotter lighting instruments of the film/video industry. Led by Chimera, the leading manufacturer of portable, collapsible lightbanks (softlights), and other companies such as Lowel, Photoflex and Westcott, the use of portable softlights has become commonplace in nearly every area of production. The soft light quality of the lightbank produces a very natural, attractive look that can be seen on many network news and entertainment programs.

The advantage to the Chimera system is that the lightbanks can be adapted to work with almost any instrument in the world—from 100 watts to 20,000 watts. All other softlight systems can work with lights of up to only 1,000 watts. Once again, the benefits of such a system come at a cost. While the smaller lightbanks and adapter rings (called Speed Rings) run only several hundred dollars, the purchase of a larger lightbank with rings and accessories can easily run well over a thousand dollars. Lowel-Light, the makers of the omnipresent Lowel lighting kit, also offers a portable softlight called the Rifa-Light. The Rifa-Light is designed with a built-in lamp, and it opens and closes like an umbrella. While this light does not offer quite the range of use that a Chimera lightbank offers, it does provide a very nice light quality and a top output of 1,000 watts at a lower price.

Recent Developments

Due to the downsizing of lighting instruments, one of the more popular products today is simply a repackaging of lights into light kits. Available from many companies, lighting kits include sturdy travel cases, light stands, and a variety of three to four Fresnels and open-faced instruments that normally range from 200 watts to 1,000 watts. Lowel-Light was perhaps the originator of traveling light kits, and now, due to the extensive use of smaller, less-powerful lights on location, many manufacturers have their version of a portable kit. Arriflex has a kit that offers one 1,000-watt open-face, two 650 Fresnels, one 300-watt light, and a Chimera lightbank that works with the 1K open-face. Add four light stands and all of the normal accessories (barndoors, scrims, etc.) in a rolling case, and you have yourself a very useful lighting kit for approximately $2,500. LTM has their version of a kit with Pepper lights (small Fresnels), but most other manufacturers do not include a lightbank. Higher-sensitivity CCD cameras have increased the use of small Fresnel instruments such as the 650-watt Peppers in location and studio video production.

Many of the newest HMI lights have been redesigned for better efficiency. Today's HMI instruments are, in general, much more efficient and smaller in size and weight. The new Arrisun 1,200-watt Plus Par, with the narrow beam lenses, produces almost three times the output as the older 1,200-watt Arri Par (see Table 12.1). Although Arri opted for better performance rather than smaller size, most manufacturers now offer smaller HMI lights with better performance. The introduction of dimmable electronic ballasts, which provide flicker-free operation for film lighting, also significantly reduced ballast weight. Dimmability in new HMI ballasts allows for quick adjustments to light output with only a slight increase in color temperature.

This downsizing of instruments and ballasts—combined with the introduction of many new, lower-wattage HMI lights—has also led to the introduction of HMI kits. The K5,600 company has had a kit of 200-watt and 400-watt HMI Pars available for several years now. In 1997, Arri is unveiling several new, smaller HMIs, including the 125-watt HMI Fresnel and the 125-watt Pocket Par. The new 125 Pocket Par is less than seven inches long and weighs only 2.6 pounds (without electronic ballast), can be powered by either AC or DC ballasts, and produces an impressive 1,170 footcandles at 10 feet (narrow beam). The price with ballast is approximately $4,400.

Table 12.1

Output of Arri HMI Par Light Compared
with New Arri 12 Plus Par

Lens	Wide	Medium	Narrow	Very Narrow
1,200 Par	425	1,500	3,250	4,500
12 Plus Par	481	1,688	6,250	14,063

Photometric Data (in footcandles at 20 feet)

Source: B. Holshevnikoff

In the fluorescent realm, the most significant factor appears to be the introduction of dimmable ballasts. Due to the nature of fluorescent lighting, once the light placement is set, it is difficult to adjust the output of the light. There is no spot or flood adjustment. Adding a dimmable ballast allows the user to make simple adjustments to the light output without moving the instrument and with little or no color shift.

Light control is perhaps one of the most important aspects of lighting. Using flags, scrims, and the barndoors on the lights allows you to selectively subtract light in any environment. Allowing light to inadvertently spill onto walls and set pieces usually produces images that can look sloppy or overlit. One of the more recent developments is a variety of products that provide light control for soft light sources. Led by Chimera and a few other manufacturers, there are now several different products, called grids or louvers, that you can use to control spill light from a soft source (Holshevnikoff, 1997). What barndoors are to hard light, grids and louvers are to soft lights. Commonplace in the photographic industry for years, these light control accessories are finally making it to the film and television industries. The beauty of these new products is that they attach directly to the front of the soft light source, so there is no need for additional stands and grip equipment, and some even fold up small enough to fit into your coat pocket.

Eggcrates, which look like large, black-metal ice cube trays, have been used for years on large studio soft lights. They are not practical, however, for location use, and they can be heavy and awkward to use. The new generation of light control devices is lightweight, and they offer complete control of the spill light. Depending on which type of soft light sources you own or use, there are honeycomb grids, louvers, and soft grids now available for many of these products (see photo), and each offers slightly different benefits and qualities.

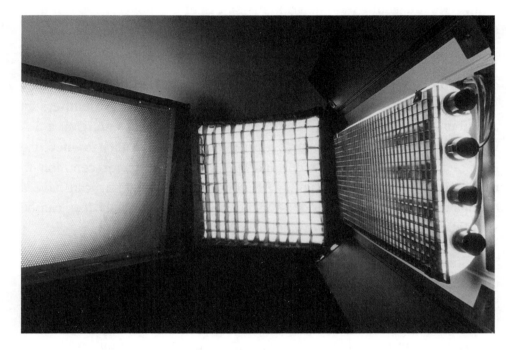

Left to right: Chimera lightbank with honeycomb grid, Lowel Rifa-Light with soft grid, Kino Flo fluorescent light with louver. Photo courtesy of Bill Holshevnikoff.

Chimera offers all three types of light control accessories, and each attaches neatly into the front recess area on the lightbanks with Velcro tabs. The honeycomb grid is a thin aluminum wafer that offers the highest level of beam-width control, and is available in varying degrees of beam spread. Although the honeycomb grids are the most expensive of these devices ($165 to $700), they offer superb light control when using lightbanks on large sets or tabletops. The only significant negative factor with the honeycombs is that they are difficult to transport.

Of nearly the same control with much better portability, both Chimera and Lowel now offer the soft, or fabric, grid. While only slightly less expensive, fabric grids set up instantly and can fold up quickly to the size of a telephone handset. Again, Chimera offers a variety of different beam width choices with their soft grids. Lowel offers the soft grid for their Rifa-Lights, which greatly enhances the uses and control of the instrument. Prior to the introduction of the soft grid, the Rifa-Light was a very handy soft light source, but it offered no simple method of controlling the spill light. With the addition of the grid, this soft light can now be used in tight spaces with good control and no need for additional grip equipment.

In the fluorescent world, all of the manufacturers offer a grid or louver device for their instruments. Kino Flo has offered a hard plastic grid (they call them louvers) since the inception of the product. Videssence offers an aluminum honeycomb grid. Fluorescent tubes, by their design, emit a diffused light, and the use of the grids greatly improves the ability to direct the light and control the beam width and spill. The one factor common to nearly all grids is a loss of light. All good things in lighting can have a down side, and the negative side to using grids is that the light loss can be significant—up to two stops of light in some cases.

The Source-4 leko light (ellipsoidal), manufactured by the ETC Corporation, has been a popular new product for both studio and location lighting. Smaller than the traditional leko light, the Source-4 uses a 575-watt tungsten lamp, but has the output of more than the older 1,000-watt units. The light also runs cooler than older units, which prevents the common problem of burning the metal patterns that are used for projecting backgrounds in film, television, and theater lighting. A major reason for the Source-4's popularity is a price tag of under $300.

For those who wish to have the flexibility to create background patterns without the use of leko lights, Chimera has introduced "Window Patterns." Used with Chimera's portable Lightform frames, this set of six mylar patterns (18" × 18", or "micro" 13" × 13") attach instantly to a black fabric and the collapsible frame to allow the user to project different patterns onto any background. Using any Fresnel or open-faced instrument, this portable pattern system can be used to project venetian or vertical blind patterns, palm fronds, tree leaves, window frame, or standard cucaloris patterns.

For a cost of approximately $350, these patterns can help to break up the bland white wall backgrounds on corporate office shoots.

In studio dimmer control systems, the solid-state technology that has been prevalent for the past five years is still the standard today. The addition of a nearly worldwide, standardized digital control signal (DMX 512 control) five years ago is probably the most significant recent improvement in dimmers. The use of a digital control signal has spawned new technology from industry leaders such as ETC (the makers of the Source 4 light), Strand, and Entertainment Technologies (ET). Older industry kings Colortran and Kliegl have fallen on difficult times.

ET, a smaller company with some very interesting new digital technology, was acquired by Rosco (gels, diffusion, and lighting products) in 1994. Their new IPS (Intelligent Power System) console works with a concept called "distributed dimmers." Rather than have a single brain center with cables to each and every light, this system relies on intelligent dimmer bars in the grid that can each run many instruments (i.e., 6 × 2.4 kilowatts per bar). A single cable connects the dimmer bars to the main control dimmer, and the operator can then pull up detailed information such as voltage and power updates, bad lamps in instruments, temperature updates on dimmer bars, and programmable auto shut-offs. The reduction in power cables with this system can save thousands of dollars on the cost of installation. RF (radio frequency) noise has been a problem with older dimmer systems as well, and ET has new "noiseless" dimmers that can be very useful for film, television, and live performance applications.

Current Status

In broadcast production, the lighting trend for many programs has been, and is currently, to use bigger, softer sources for much of the program lighting. Fluorescent lighting and soft sources such as Chimera lightbanks and Rifa-Lights are being used by hundreds of stations and on many network programs (CNN *PrimeTime*, *60 Minutes*, *20/20*, and ABC's *World News Tonight*). There are tremendous advantages to working with softer lighting. Soft light is more forgiving, and the talent can look and feel their best on camera. In addition, softer light usually means flatter lighting, which directors like because it allows them freedom to shoot the set from many different angles. Unfortunately, without careful installation, softer lighting can also produce flat, visually-uninteresting images. Care must be taken to keep some level of shadow form on the talent and set pieces, and, to do that, one must have proper light placement and utilize some form of light control. This is where the new grids and louvers become invaluable accessories.

For location productions, smaller trucks and crews are producing more and more programming. Crews of three to four people are traveling with a light kit, several light control accessories, and a digital Betacam system to create some powerful imagery in reduced time. Smaller, more-efficient lighting instruments are making the production of many lower-budget programs possible, while making the production of larger-budget programs easier and more fun for us, as viewers, to watch.

In many states now, it has become illegal (for fire safety reasons) to tie-in for power (tap into the main power lines behind the breaker box). The trend of using smaller, less-powerful instruments could not be better timed for this new safety guideline. If the production still demands the use of larger, more powerful instruments, the use of a portable generator is now required.

Factors to Watch

As mentioned at the beginning of this chapter, new technologies in the lighting industry have been slow to evolve. Currently, lighting manufacturers are utilizing computer design technologies to improve light output, reduce weight, and increase durability and heat resistance. New "smart" technologies are being implemented into power and dimming control systems so that different sources can be utilized within a system without having to manually power levels and controls.

Look for continued cross-over and sharing of ideas and technologies between still and motion media lighting experts and stage and concert lighting professionals. Even architectural lighting professionals have contributed useful ideas and products to the film and video industries. With new, light-sensitive film stocks and television cameras, many of the perceived boundaries of the production world are being re-established each year. The implementation of digital HDTV may change many aspects of television production and broadcasting, but the lighting for high-definition imagery will remain basically the same as it is today.

Bibliography

Box, H. C. (1993). *Set lighting technician's handbook.* Boston: Focal Press.

Brown, B. (1996). *Motion picture and video lighting.* Boston: Focal Press.

Ferncase, R. K. (1995). *Film and video lighting and concepts.* Boston: Focal Press.

Fitt, B., & Thornley, J. (1992). *Lighting by design.* Boston: Focal Press.

Holshevnikoff, B. (1995a, May). The HMI Par light. *Video Systems,* 66-67.

Holshevnikoff, B. (1995b, July). The new fluorescents. *Video Systems,* 52-53.

Holshevnikoff, B. (1997, January). Light control for soft light. *Video Systems,* 71, 74-75.

Lowel, R. (1994). *Matters of light and depth.* Broad Street Books.

Malkiewicz, K. (1986). *Film lighting.* New York: Prentice Hall.

Millerson, G. (1991). *The technique of lighting for television and film* (3rd ed.). Boston: Focal Press.

IV

Transmission Technologies

In addition to production and reception, a fundamental element of the broadcast triad is transmission. While the term "broadcasting" still indicates a signal transmitted through the air, new technologies are rapidly transforming the way program content is reaching listeners and viewers. For this reason, we have added a section dedicated just to transmission technologies.

Chapter 13 examines the comparatively slow rate of change in radio transmission technology compared with recent developments in digital television standards. However, radio technology is also being transformed by new innovations in digital broadcasting. The FCC is planning an auction of digital audio radio service (DARS) spectrum in the spring of 1997, and there is hope that this service may finally get off the ground in the next two years. A number of other promising digital systems are examined in the chapter, and it also takes a look at the burgeoning area of Internet radio broadcasting. Radio transmission over the 'Net has been hampered by bandwidth, server, and software limitations, but new developments in multicast technology hold great promise for streaming real-time audio from a station server to thousands of listeners at the same time. The radio transmission systems of the future are going to be an interesting mix of wired and wireless technologies, all of which are addressed in this chapter.

Chapter 14 offers a view of the atypical TV home of the near future with every possible transmission route included. It includes analyses of video services provided by over-the-air broadcasters, cable companies, direct broadcast satellite services, telephone companies, and even possibly the local power company. All of them would like a share of the local cable monopoly on service provision, and all of them are making plans to convert their analog transmission systems to digital technology. It is a tumultuous time in the television transmission business, and the chapter examines the technological, economic, and political issues involved.

The long-debated merger of television and digital content is already here with the arrival of technologies such as WebTV, and the creation of a U.S. digital television transmission standard will accelerate the process. No one knows what the effect will be on television or Internet content, but it seems clear that channel surfing will take on a entirely new meaning as a result. Descriptions of the future "500-channel" broadcast/cable universe may turn out to be very short-sighted—the ultimate limit may be the aggregate number of audio- and video-capable servers connected to the Internet. This digital merger may hold as many surprises for content providers as for viewers.

13

Radio Transmission

David Sedman

One of the major stories in recent broadcast history was the FCC action bringing television into the digital transmission age. The support for an advanced television system came not only from the broadcast industry and the consumer electronics companies, but also from the Hollywood and computer industries. U.S. radio broadcasting, on the other hand, remains a primarily analog-transmitted, AM and FM medium. It is unlikely that the industry will receive any technological advice or stimulus from outside forces as it struggles to decide when and how to enter the digital era. One might even question why radio is worthy of discussion in a book devoted to cutting-edge broadcast technology. Although technological developments in radio transmission today are mundane, acting primarily to enhance the current AM/FM system, experts continue perfecting systems which will bring radio improved sound and dynamic new features.

Background

Guglielmo Marconi, generally considered the inventor of radio, first transmitted telegraphic dots and dashes without the use of wires in the 1890s. In the early 20th century, tremendous advances led to radio telephony that allowed voice and music to be transmitted without wires. During the 20th century, the commercial radio industry has been served by two transmission bands: amplitude modulation (AM) and frequency modulation (FM). Radio is also transmitted in short wave (SW) and high frequency (HF). The first radio stations were transmitted only in AM and have long suffered from electrical interference and limitations of fidelity. FM, developed in the 1930s and 1940s, provided a superior sounding service but was limited in range. The two bands continue to coexist in contemporary radio. However, FM has overtaken AM in attracting audiences because it is ideally suited to music format radio.

Consumer audio technology introduced over the past 40 years has helped spur broadcast engineers into developing areas to augment and enhance a station's transmission. The increased use of stereophonic systems in the 1950s and 1960s helped lead to more FM stereo broadcasts and, during the 1980s and 1990s, AM broadcasters have also been making the transformation from monaural to stereo transmission. Four-channel, quadraphonic home systems of the 1960s led to experimentation with Quad-FM. Because quad home systems were not adopted by a critical mass of consumers, they disappeared from the consumer electronics marketplace, and experiments with Quad-FM were discontinued. When the digital compact disc replaced the analog vinyl record in the 1980s, many predicted that digital audio broadcasting transmission would replace analog systems by the early 1990s. This has not been the case in the United States or in most other countries. However, field tests and experiments continue with the hope of bringing digital transmission to the radio industry.

Some have become frustrated by radio's slow technological progress. Major changes in radio service are challenging to integrate. To be successful, a new service generally requires four levels of adoption:

(1)   Approval by a governing body (such as the FCC in the United States).

(2)   Acceptance by the broadcast station.

(3)   Consent from the consumer electronics industry to design and market a new technology.

(4)   Adoption by the mass buying public.

This has not stopped engineers and inventors from continuing to design technology to improve upon radio's quality and scope.

Recent Developments

There are three basic categories that describe contemporary technological trends in the area of radio transmission. The first two categories view radio for what it is: one of the last remaining analog-delivered media. The first category is enhancements to present-day transmissions, and the second includes supplements designed to provide new services to radio audience members. The third category, new delivery modes, looks to the future when the industry moves toward digital transmission.

Enhancements: Extending the AM Band

Someday, AM radio stations may gravitate to the digital domain and be able to compete more effectively with their FM counterparts. Because this potential shift will not take place in the 20th century in the United States, current AM broadcasters have adopted some stopgap approaches to improve their service. One of these occurred in 1996 when the FCC (1996a) moved 83 stations from crowded frequencies on the AM dial (between 535 MHz and 1605 MHz) to the expanded portion of the band between 1605 MHz and 1705 MHz. This move provided stations with fewer interference problems because these were the first U.S. stations to occupy this portion of the spectrum.

Supplements: SCS and RDS

The concept of supplemental audio services is common to FM radio. FM broadcasters utilize sidebands of their transmission signal to feed additional services to specially-equipped receivers. These subsidiary communications services (SCS) were instituted in the 1950s. Current uses for SCS include reading services for the visually impaired and background music heard in stores and office buildings.

The latest use of sidebands is for the delivery of data known as the radio data system (RDS) or RBDS (radio broadcast data system). RDS transmits information to specially-equipped receivers, sometimes called "smart radios" (Ammons, 1995). The information can include the positioning statement of the radio station, the artist and song title of a musical selection currently playing, traffic and weather alerts, and advertiser information. Smart radios could also be programmed to turn on a set to receive an emergency message and to automatically change to a station with the same format if the original station's signal became weak.

Although RDS has been used in Europe since the 1980s, it has diffused slowly in the United States. Because only a small percentage of radio stations are transmitting with RDS, there is little consumer knowledge of or demand for the service. Consequently, few consumer electronics makers are producing RDS hardware. In order to stimulate interest on the part of broadcasters, the Electronic Industry Association offered to share the cost of buying transmission equipment with stations in the top 25 U.S. markets if the station committed itself to the use and promotion of RDS services. More than 700 stations made a commitment to use RDS in 1997.

As is the case with all new broadcast technologies, the cost of the hardware starts out very high and, as the technology diffuses, the cost of equipment goes down. The first generation of receivers cost $25,000. In 1995, the receivers cost $7,000 each, and by 1996, the receivers cost $2,700. The technology appears headed in the right direction. RDS signals have a potential audience of more than 30 million listeners, and RDS equipment is being offered on some models of 1998 automobiles. For the technology to succeed with a critical mass of adopters, however, the price of the equipment must continue downward, and the services will have to increase.

New Delivery Modes: The Internet

Radio stations face competition from Webcasters which have no license but have inaugurated audio service on the Internet. Not surprisingly, radio stations have decided to take a high profile approach to the Internet. The number of U.S. radio broadcasters that have home pages on the Internet has gone from a handful in 1994 to more than 3,000 by spring 1997. The figure grows each week (BRS, 1997). A number of these stations (about 400 at the time of publication) also provide audio samples of their broadcasts or simulcast their services on the Internet. Full-service Web-stations use applications such as RealAudio or Microsoft's ActiveMovie Streaming Format (ASF) to transmit their service 24 hours a day.

The fundamental problem with present streaming technologies on the Web is that they are fundamentally "unicast" technologies that feed programming from station servers to listeners, one at a time, limiting the number who might be able to listen in. A consortium of computer software, hardware, and networking companies, known as the Internet Protocol Multicasting Initiative (IPMI), is working on a "multicast" standard (Van Tassel, 1997). Multicasting would stream radio or audio programming from source servers over dedicated Internet lines to service providers who would then pass it along to thousands of their customers at a time, eliminating the present unicast bottleneck. The success of a multicast standard could transform global broadcasting, making it possible for listeners in Hong Kong to easily access a Chicago alternative FM radio station without preempting excessive Internet bandwidth.

Digital Audio Broadcasting

The most anticipated transformation of radio technology will take place when digital audio broadcasting (DAB) becomes the predominant transmission mode. DAB is also referred to as DAR (digital audio radio) and digital sound broadcasting. Stations which use digital audio technologies such as CDs, minidiscs (MDs), digital audio workstations (DAWS), and digital cart players will be able to maintain the digital nature of their audio signals. However, DAB presents a number of problems. Stations must incur the costs of new transmitters, while the buying public will have to buy receivers capable of picking up DAB. If DAB were to be implemented in the United States just after the inauguration of the advanced television system, the public might be hesitant to support yet another new technology. A survey conducted in 1996 found that only 31% of respondents were interested in having a digital radio in their car (CEMA, 1996).

Beyond the consumer-related issues are questions as to which technical standard might best serve the radio industry in the 21st century. One such question is whether DAB should be satellite-fed or terrestrially broadcast. Satellite downlinks have provided stations with audio programming since the 1970s. More recently, satellite-delivered digital audio services have become widely available on cable TV and direct broadcast satellite systems. In 1995, the FCC authorized spectrum for direct-satellite digital audio radio service (DARS) in the United States. Congress ordered the FCC to begin auctioning DARS spectrum in the spring of 1997. The Congressional Budget Office predicted that the interest in DARS was great and that the auctions, when completed, would generate about $3 billion (Fleming, 1996). If such a system were instituted, consumers would have the opportunity to purchase satellite receivers for their homes and, possibly, their cars to receive the service.

Terrestrial DAB is the more imminent possibility for radio broadcasters. Three types of terrestrial DAB have attracted industry support: "in-band on-channel" (IBOC), "in-band adjacent-channel" (IBAC), and "out-of-band" which requires a new spectrum band (Jurgen, 1996). The easiest system to inaugurate would be an IBOC system, which would leave all stations on the same frequencies that they presently occupy. It would also allow users of current analog radio sets to continue using them even after IBOC service was begun.

Unlike a number of countries that have made the transition to the L-band for DAB, the United States is hoping to find an acceptable IBOC system. The two IBOC systems under consideration in the United States by USA Digital Radio and AT&T were withdrawn from field tests during the summer of 1996. Although development continues on an improved IBOC system, no field tests have been scheduled at the time of publication.

IBAC systems also leave FM broadcasters in their current broadcast slots. They allow broadcasters to transmit digitally in adjacent sidebands. However, no IBAC systems have been developed that would allow for digital AM broadcasts. The IBAC proposal under consideration in the United

States is by Amati Communications and AT&T. It was one of only three systems which survived the field-testing process in 1996 (Meadows, 1997).

Out-of-band service would lead to the obsolescence of current radio sets if broadcasters discontinued analog service. The advantage of out-of-band is that engineers are not trying to "retrofit" an old technology. Instead, a newer system generally allows for greater freedom and a wider range of services. The out-of-band service that has become a de facto standard in Europe, Canada, Mexico, and many other countries is known as Eureka 147. Standardizing Eureka 147 in the United States would lead to the end of IBOC and IBAC work. It would also foster compatibility between the United States, our neighbors to the north and south, and other nations that have already adopted the system.

Factors to Watch

A New Economy of Scale

With more than 12,000 radio stations in the United States, a concern about widespread adoption of new radio broadcasting technology is that individual stations might not have the financial clout to institute changes. Unprofitable years for many radio stations in the late 1980s and early 1990s led to FCC ownership rule modifications which allowed competing stations to combine personnel and broker programming time through LMAs (local marketing agreements). In 1992, the FCC also eased its duopoly rule which had long prevented an owner from holding more than one AM or FM station in a given market.

The FCC rules allowed stations to streamline their operations, and many stations began to rely heavily on network-delivered programming instead of creating their own locally-originated shows. The rule changes helped radio return to profitability in the 1990s. Total advertising revenues for U.S. radio stations totaled $11.47 billion in 1995, up 8% from the previous year (Radio revenues, 1996). The national and network revenue in radio, alone, totaled $1.9 billion in 1995 (Petrozzello, 1996b). The economics were so robust that the market value of radio-related stocks increased an average of 85% between February 1995 and February 1996 (Petrozzello, 1996a).

The profits and reliance on national programming should increase as the Telecommunications Act of 1996 repealed ownership limits on the number of radio stations a single licensee could own. Furthermore, the FCC relaxed limitations on the number of stations an entity could own in a single market (FCC, 1996b).[1] As a result, radio group owners will continue to buy more stations, and consolidation within the industry will rapidly continue. During 1996, radio station transactions became a multibillion dollar business, with transaction totals up more than 400% from the previous year (Changing hands, 1996). By contrast, the total radio transactions for 1991 totaled less than $1 billion (Ditingo, 1995).

Ever-expanding group owners should have more financial buying clout when it comes to buying innovative technology, and it is expected that they will make "group buys" for their stations. In addition, some group owners already have direct ties to the innovations being tested and, therefore, might be more interested in adopting new technology. Equipment makers have already begun reporting increased sales of solid-state radio transmitters thanks to the new mega-radio chains (Petrozzello, 1996b). The adoption of new solid-state transmitters is a signal of purchasing power and a move away from tube-based models; more important, however, these major analog transmitter purchases may signify a corporate perspective that digital audio broadcasting is many years away from coming into existence.

Testing New Radio Technology

Three subcarrier services were tested in 1996 and 1997:

- The NHK FM Subcarrier Information System (FMSS) known as the Digital DJ.

- The Seiko High Speed Data System (HSDS).

- Mitre's Subcarrier Traffic Information Channel (STIC).

---

[1] In radio markets with more than 45 stations, an owner can hold licenses of up to eight commercial radio stations, of which not more than five can be in the same service (AM or FM). In markets with 30 to 44 stations, they can own seven stations, but not more than four in the same service. In markets with 15 to 29 stations, they may own six stations, but not more than four in the same service. In markets with fewer than 15 stations, they may own five stations, but not more than three in the same service and not more than 50% of the stations in that market.

HSDS would allow stations to offer data such as stock quotes and sports news on a variety of specially-equipped receivers, including radios, personal data assistants, computers, and wrist watches. The results of these tests were scheduled to be released as this went to press, as was a NAB study on what percentage of stations were interested in using these and other subcarrier services (Rusk, 1997).

It is obvious that there is great potential for a new, vibrant radio system, perhaps utilizing the Internet as an alternative transmission medium. Unfortunately, much uncertainty presently exists in the realm of radio transmission. When new transmission standards are in place, the industry should have a clearer vision of what radio service will be like in the 21st century.

Bibliography

Ammons, B. (1995, September). *RBDS for your station*. [On-line]. Available: http://www.aloha.com/~cpiengrs/rbds.htm.

BRS Radio Consultants. (1997, January 12). *Commercial radio stations on the Web*. [On-line]. Available: http://brsradio.com/.

Changing hands. (1996, December 30). *Broadcasting & Cable*, 20.

Consumer Electronics Manufacturers Association. (1996, April 15). *Consumers want CD-quality radio*. [On-line]. Available: http://www.cemacity.org/.

Ditingo, V. (1995). *The remaking of radio*. Boston: Focal Press.

FCC. (1992). *Revision of radio rules and policies*. Washington, DC: U.S. Government Printing Office.

FCC. (1996a). *Mass Media Bureau announces revised expanded AM broadcast band improvement factors and allotment plan*. Washington, DC: U.S. Government Printing Office.

FCC. (1996b). *FCC revises national multiple radio ownership rule*. [NM 96-12]. Washington, DC: U.S. Government Printing Office.

Fleming, H. (1996, October 7). DARS auctions will help underwrite federal agencies. *Broadcasting & Cable*, 20.

Jurgen, R. (1996, March). Broadcasting with digital audio. *IEEE Spectrum*, 52-59.

Meadows, L. (1997, January 8). NAB waits while IBOC readied. *Radio World*, 1, 6.

Petrozzello, D. (1996a, March 25). Riding gain. *Broadcasting & Cable*, 56.

Petrozzello, D. (1996b, June 3). Radio posts solid sales of solid-state. *Broadcasting & Cable*, 74-75.

Consumer Electronics Manufacturers Association. (1997, January 2). *RDS stations across the U.S.* [On-line]. Available: http://www.cemacity.org/.

Radio revenues up 8%. (1996, February 19). *Radio online*. [On-line serial.] Available: http://www.radio-online.com/.

Rusk, B. (1997, January 22). NRSC nearing end of HSDS lab tests. *Radio World*, 1, 11.

Van Tassel, J. (1997, January 27). Multicasting promoted to improve Webcasts. *Broadcasting & Cable*, 64.

14

Television Transmission

Peter B. Seel

After three decades of relatively little change in the fundamental technology of television transmission, the 1990s represent an era of turbulence in the status quo that has all TV service providers looking over their shoulders. The cable television industry has perhaps reached a high-water mark in terms of market share as alternative delivery services such as direct broadcast satellite (DBS) grow rapidly by drawing away their customers. Telco competition has yet to make much of a dent in the subscriber share of cable or DBS, but the regional Bell operating companies (RBOCs) state that providing video services is still an important part of their long-term strategies. The Federal Communications Commission (FCC) is actively promoting competition in the provision of television programming by drafting new rules based upon the groundwork laid by the Telecommunications Act of 1996. In the first major rewrite of telecommunications law since 1934, Congress encouraged the entry of telco competitors in the video marketplace, but mandated significant hurdles they must leap prior to entry in the television services arena.

The 1996 Act also awarded digital transmission spectrum to all U.S. broadcasters for the purpose of transmitting a second simulcast channel of advanced television (ATV) programming. In the most significant change in American terrestrial broadcasting since the introduction of color television in the 1950s, the advent of digital ATV transmission portends the gradual merger of computer and video technologies into a system that has the potential to transform television content and related viewing habits. This sea change in broadcast technology will be addressed in greater detail in the Recent Developments section.

Background

Figure 14.1 shows the typical American home with all of the possible signal paths into the household. This home is atypical in that it has *every* possible signal path available at the present time. The conventional over-the-air antenna symbolizes the landscape of the 1950s and 1960s with skylines spiked with backyard towers topped by large aluminum antennas. The cable entering the home from the antenna was unusual in that it plugged right into the back of the television set without any VCRs or cable boxes in the signal path as is common today.

TV antennas became a rarer sight in suburbia as green cable "mushrooms" in front yards replaced terrestrial antennas in the 1970s and 1980s. The cable feed to the household is called a "drop," as it is an offshoot of the main feeder line running down the street in front (or in back) of the home. The cable extends to a set-top box that decodes the signal and provides 40 to 80 channels of analog programming. The cable television industry is in the midst of a massive conversion from analog to digital technology along the entire signal path from the national network uplink all the way to the subscriber's set-top box. At the local level, coaxial cable is being replaced by fiber optic trunk lines that extend to neighborhood nodes (fiber-to-the-node systems) to expand system bandwidth and offer the potential for two-way interactivity between subscribers and the system headend.

Figure 14.1

Television Transmission Routes into the Home

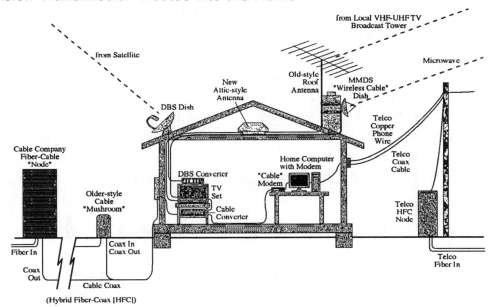

Source: Peter B. Seel

On the roof of the home is a DBS dish pulling in broadcast signals from a direct broadcast satellite "parked" in geosynchronous orbit 22,300 miles above the United States (Pavlik, 1996). The dish focuses the signal on a receiver module, and it is passed into the home via coaxial cable and down-converted at another set-top box near the television set. The signal stays in digital form from the uplink dish all the way to the set-top, being converted to analog only just before it passes into the TV set. Note that there is another terrestrial antenna in the attic, but it is a more modern version designed to be used in conjunction with the DBS dish. One significant drawback to DBS services is that they provide programming on a national basis, and by law, cannot provide local or network programming if it is available via terrestrial broadcast. For this reason, DBS users must hook up an antenna or subscribe to basic cable to receive local television channels.

A copper twisted-pair telephone cable enters the home, providing telephone service and a modem connection to the Internet for the home computer. Although the Internet was originally a text- and data-oriented network, the development of the World Wide Web and graphical Internet browsers since 1990 have transformed Net content into a multimedia potpourri of sites with color images, animation, embedded real-time data, audio, and now video. The addition of this data-intensive multimedia content sent high-end users scurrying for telco services such as ISDN that can download content far faster than the standard 28.8 Kb/s modem. National service providers such as Sprint and AT&T have been expanding their fiber optic backbone networks at a record pace, but they are have having difficulty keeping up with user demand for greater bandwidth. Many of the RBOCs had grandiose plans to provide video on demand programming to their customers by the year 2000, but have scaled them back in the face of enormous construction costs and uncertain consumer demand. However, in some areas, they are installing hybrid fiber/coax (HFC) systems similar to those being installed by cable companies.

Some of the RBOCs such as Pacific Telesis have turned to multichannel, multipoint distribution service (MMDS) technology as a short-term solution to providing video services to their customers without having to bury wires in the ground (Martin, 1996). MMDS utilizes microwave signals beamed from a neighborhood tower to a small dish or antenna on the roof of a home or apartment (see Figure 14.1). The primary advantage of this technology is that it is relatively inexpensive to install compared with the cost of burying coaxial cable under streets and yards. The downside is that transmission requires a clear line-of-sight from tower to home, and this distance can be circumscribed by hilly terrain and tall buildings. Existing MMDS services are also in the process of converting to digital transmission technology to remain competitive with their cable and telco counterparts (Martin, 1996).

There are other methods of getting a television signal from a transmitter or headend to the home, and even local power companies have examined the feasibility of using their networks of towers and electrical lines as a platform for providing video and data services to their customers.

The net result of all this activity by television programming providers is that consumers have more service options than in the days of hooking up a rooftop antenna or waiting for cable to pass their homes. These options will grow in the future with the rollout of telco video services, an expansion in the number of DBS providers, and the evolution of Internet technologies that permit real-time delivery of high-quality audio and video content.

Recent Developments

The analog-to-digital transition outlined in Chapter 2 is influencing every aspect of television production, transmission, and reception. In the transmission process, digital compression allows a typical fivefold expansion in cable channel capacity, or it can be the basis for the electronic alchemy that permits a terrestrial broadcaster to shoehorn an HDTV signal into a conventional 6 MHz channel assignment. To comprehend the recent changes taking place in television transmission technology, it is perhaps most useful to address them industry by industry.

Cable Television

The cable TV industry transformed itself from prototypical "mom and pop" entrepreneurs who sold their neighbors improved television reception from crude mountaintop antennas via coaxial cable strung from house to house. Today, cable is a global multibillion-dollar industry that is still the most dominant television service provider in the United States and is growing rapidly in Asia and Europe as well. In America, cable passes 96% of all U.S. households, and 64% of them subscribe to some level of service (Brown, 1996). Since the passage of the Telecommunications Act of 1996, there has been a great deal of consolidation in the cable business, as smaller companies were bought out by large multiple system operators (MSOs) seeking the critical mass needed to fend off potential RBOC competitors.

Cable operators have been expanding the channel capacity of their systems not only to provide more pay-per-view services such as movies on demand, but also to add new two-way data services. Cable giant TCI launched a new digital transmission service in late 1996 called Headend In The Sky (HITS) that will compress over 100 channels of programming at their uplink site in Denver, beam it up to a satellite, down to a local cable system, and out to the subscriber in compressed form (Tele-Communications, Inc., 1996). At the customer's set-top, the signal is decompressed and converted to analog form. This form of digital compression will give local TCI affiliates the ability to dramatically expand system capacity without having to rebuild their entire systems. However, substantial redesign of cable systems will be necessary to provide the switching and return-path capability for telephone and interactive media services. Cable systems were originally designed for one-way signal flow from headend to customer, not for customer-to-customer communication.

Beyond voice telephony, one area of significant potential growth for cable companies is providing wide-bandwidth Internet access. Cable companies have placed million-unit orders for desktop cable modems that can feed data from a coaxial cable to the home computer or digital television at 10 Mb/s—1,000 times the data rate of the still widely-used 9.6 Kb/s telco modem (Freed, 1997). This data "firehose" will remove one bandwidth bottleneck that slows the distribution of video and audio programming via the Internet (other issues on this topic are discussed below). The key point is that the very high transmission capacity of coaxial cable offers a significant competitive advantage in the Internet service area to cable operators when compared with conventional telco system capacity.

Direct Broadcast Satellite (DBS) Services

DBS services have a key technical advantage over their competitors—their transmission signal path is already all-digital. Their focus in the past two years has been on expanding the numbers of channels beyond the 30 to 40 that most services offered at the start. Digital compression is being used in this market to expand transmission capacity to over 100 channels. Satellite dishes have been used by consumers in rural areas ever since broadcast and cable networks moved to satellite transmission in the 1970s—over four million of these large (typically eight feet in diameter) C-band dishes are still in use today (Jessell, 1996a).

The launch of a high-powered satellite by USSB and DirecTV in 1994 made it possible to shrink receiving dishes to only 18 inches, a significant advantage that reduced system prices from thousands of dollars to about $600. In one of the most successful product introductions in history, sales of small dishes jumped from 600,000 units sold in 1994 to over 1.6 million in 1995 (Brown, 1996). The number of DBS systems tripled again in 1996, with analysts predicting six million subscribers by the end of the year, and perhaps 20 million by 2000 (McConville, 1996). Reduced hardware prices have been a key factor in consumer acceptance of this technology; it is now possible to purchase a complete system (without installation) for under $100, if the consumer also buys a year of programming for $300 (McConville, 1996).

The skies over America are becoming crowded with broadcast satellites as another media conglomerate prepares to enter the market in 1997. American Sky Broadcasting (ASkyB), a joint venture of MCI Communications and News Corporation, bid $682.5 million in a 1996 FCC auction for the last orbital slot capable of transmitting to the entire United States (Ashworth, 1997). Both companies are huge players in telecommunications (MCI was recently purchased by British Telecommunications, and News Corporation is the parent of Fox Broadcasting), and they are expected to heat up the competition for DBS subscribers in the next two years.

The beauty of DBS transmission is that it is wireless—no cables to bury under streets or to hang from telco poles. The downside to this mode is that space can be a harsh and unforgiving environment. At 6:15 A.M. (EST) on January 11, 1997, AT&T suddenly lost contact with the Telstar 401 satellite that was a vital bridge for network television transmission. As AT&T technicians scrambled to reroute their broadcast customers to other satellites, it was conjectured that Telstar 401 had collided with a piece of orbiting space junk at high speed—one hazard that terrestrial broadcasters do not have to worry about (Dickson, 1997; Katz, 1997).

Telco Video

The enthusiasm shared by the RBOCs in the early 1990s for their own broadband networks capable of carrying video programming has been tempered in the latter half of the decade by the enormity of the costs involved. Some of the RBOCs have sought economies of scale by merging, as have Pacific Telesis and SBC Communications (formerly Southwestern Bell) and NYNEX with Bell Atlantic. Elaborate broadband trial projects have been postponed, scaled-back, or even canceled.

Most symbolic of the turmoil engendered by these telco mergers was the fate of Tele-TV. The company was created with great fanfare in October 1994 by a consortium of Bell Atlantic, NYNEX, and Pacific Telesis to promote the development of interactive broadband programming and technology. Former CBS executive Howard Stringer was hired as chairman, and Hollywood media mavens at Creative Artists Agency were retained as consultants to advise on assembling entertainment packages. After sinking more than $500 million in the company over a two-year period, the partners dissolved it in late 1996 after the Pactel/SBC merger forced a showdown on the future of Tele-TV (Cauley, 1996). The three companies discovered, in a very expensive way, the intense level of competition that exists in the provision of video services to American households.

Bell Atlantic and NYNEX have since decided to pursue DBS program distribution, while Pacific Telesis purchased MMDS provider Cross Country Cable in the Los Angeles area as a way to jump-start their entry into the video market. MMDS operators were given permission by the FCC in mid-1996 to convert their operations to digital transmission technology (Colman, 1996). American telephone companies may someday offer broadband video services to consumers on a widespread, systematic basis, but it may not be before 2000.

Internet Broadcasting

A great deal of interest has emerged since 1995 concerning the notion of using the Internet as a "broadcast" medium for audio and video programming. This has been fueled by the development of software-based technologies such as Progressive Technologies' RealAudio that permit the real-time "streaming" of a radio program over the Net. Rather than waiting for the entire file to download prior to playback, streaming technology allows the listener to hear the program as it is being transmitted from the source server. VDOnet has developed a similar technology for streaming video in real time, as have several other companies (Venditto, 1996). The catch is that the programming is not being broadcast in the conventional sense, but is "unicast" from the server to a limited number of listeners or viewers with a server connection. If the server has a capacity of 100 listeners, that is the maximum number of users at any given time.

As noted in Chapter 13, an Internet Protocol Multicasting Initiative group was formed in January 1997 to develop multicasting standards that would permit thousands of listeners to hear the same radio broadcast without bringing the Internet to a halt in the process (Van Tassel, 1997). Multicasting providers would use a dedicated part of the Internet infrastructure to deliver programming to on-line services and service providers who would then pass it along to their individual customers, bypassing the unicast bottleneck. If this technology is successful, it has the potential to transform radio and television distribution systems in the United States and throughout the world. Because the Net is an international network, it may be possible for radio listeners to have access to any of the world's stations if they offer multicast transmission. The limitations are the bandwidth constraints imposed by the Internet and the exponential growth in the annual number of users.

Terrestrial Broadcasting

The big news for terrestrial broadcasters is that the FCC has finally decided on a digital television standard. After almost 10 years of working on a new advanced television standard, on December 24, 1996, the FCC decided that the nation would convert to a new system of digital television transmission that is completely incompatible with the existing NTSC system of cameras, VTRs, switchers, and television sets (Brinkley, 1996). They proposed that every existing broadcast station in America be awarded a second channel on which to *simulcast* advanced television programming over a 15-year period. Under the plan, viewers with digital televisions will watch programming on the new channel, while those with older-model sets will see the same program on the NTSC channel. It is expected that widescreen digital television sets will go on sale in 1998 at a price that is $1,000 to $1,500 above that of present television models (Brinkley, 1996).

A number of key issues related to the transition from analog to digital television broadcasting remain unresolved as of this writing. The Clinton administration has proposed shortening the 15-year simulcast period in order to help balance the federal budget, as the administration anticipates raising billions of dollars in revenue from auctioning analog television spectrum being vacated by broadcasters (Dupagne & Seel, 1997). For similar reasons, many in Congress have proposed that broadcasters should have to pay for their new digital channels, either with cash or with increased public service obligations.

Indications in early 1997 are that broadcasters will be allowed only five to 10 years of simulcasting analog and digital signals before being forced to give up their analog spectrum. But, as the day approaches when all analog transmitters will be turned off, expect viewers who have hundreds—or thousands—of dollars invested in analog television sets to successfully lobby their representatives to delay the demise of analog television broadcasting. At that point, viewers still using NTSC televisions will need a digital-to-analog converter box for each set in the home, and the estimated $200 cost per converter may be too much for some viewers to pay.

In the meantime, U.S. television networks are making plans to begin ATV transmission in 1998 as the first digital sets go on sale. The FCC awarded the first experimental HDTV licenses to:

- WRC-TV (NBC) and WETA-TV (PBS) in Washington, D.C.

- WRAL-TV (CBS) in Raleigh, North Carolina.

- WCBS-TV (CBS) in New York.

- KOMO-TV (ABC) and KCTS-TV (PBS) in Seattle.

More stations are receiving licenses every month. The pioneer digital broadcasters will be setting up ATV master control rooms that parallel their existing NTSC operations (see Figure 14.2). They will feed digital programming to a special ATV transmitter and antenna at their tower site—in many cases, the ATV antenna can be attached to the existing broadcast tower. In 1998, when the national networks begin transmitting ATV programming to their local broadcast affiliates, most of these stations will simply pass-through this signal from their downlink dish to the transmitter. During the 15-year conversion period, stations will gradually produce more of their local programming in the ATV standard (down-converting it to NTSC for local simulcast). The cost for station network signal pass-through has been estimated at $1 million, and complete station conversion at $10 million to $12 million (Jessell, 1996).

ATV channel assignments and transmitter power levels are two of the key issues that still need to be resolved concerning ATV transmission. In 1996, the FCC published a tentative Table of Allotments outlining the ATV spectrum assignments to existing broadcasters (McConnell, 1996), but the commission will not make a final decision on these assignments until April 1997 (Brinkley, 1996). The FCC originally proposed that all ATV assignments were to be made in the UHF band, but has since made plans to assign them in the VHF spectrum using channels seven through 13 and in the UHF spectrum between channels 14 and 51 (FCC, 1996). The commission wants to retain UHF channels 60 through 69 to auction to other telecommunications users, but broadcasters have vociferously protested this plan.

A potential conflict between VHF and UHF broadcasters over transmission power levels was resolved in early 1997 by an industry compromise that will allow UHF stations to boost their assigned ATV power levels for two years (1997-1999), while capping VHF advanced television transmission levels (McConnell, 1997). Some UHF broadcasters had complained that the assigned power levels would give an unfair power advantage to VHF stations in terms of their ATV transmission contour.

The national conversion to digital television transmission is a significant event for the United States. It will be very costly for broadcasters and consumers, but the transition represents the first true merger between computing and television. The new standard may permit TV viewers to easily access the Internet and will facilitate the display of television programming on computer screens. The displays will be scaleable from quarter-screen windows on a desktop PC display to wall-size HDTV images accompanied by six-channel surround sound. It will be interesting to see what types of hybrid programming emerge from the merger of broadcast television, computer gaming, and the Internet.

Figure 14.2
ATV Simulcasting

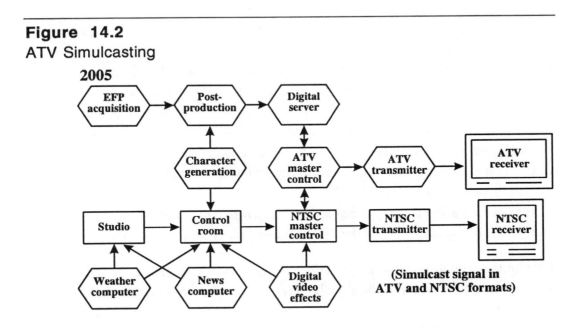

Source: Peter B. Seel

Factors to Watch

One key factor to track will be the rate at which national television networks ramp-up production of ATV programming. Since 70% of prime-time television programming is presently originated on 35mm widescreen motion picture film, transferring this material to HDTV videotape for network playback will be a relatively simple process (Stow, 1993). Warner Brothers, along with several other Hollywood studios, have been filming television series such as *ER* in widescreen aspect ratios since 1993 (cropping to 4:3 for broadcast), anticipating that recording the original program on widescreen film would increase the syndication value of the programs (Cookson, 1995).

It is expected that many network owned-and-operated affiliates in large cities will be among the first stations to convert to ATV broadcasting, but the more significant trend to follow will be the rate that stations in smaller cities adopt ATV pass-through and local origination. In the ATV transition, the deciding factor in switching off the nation's NTSC transmitters is going to be when the *last* U.S. station makes the conversion—not the first.

The simulcast transition to ATV broadcasting will also affect every cable system in the country. Although the issue has yet to be resolved by the FCC, cable companies may be required to retransmit both the NTSC and ATV versions of each station's programming. As noted above, cable companies have been adopting digital compression technology to expand channel capacity. Much of this added capacity will be needed to carry ATV simulcast versions of existing channels. Not only must they carry two channels for every broadcaster, they will need to have the capacity to simulcast all cable channels—CNN, A&E, ESPN, HBO—as well. The notion of a 500-channel cable system is not so far-fetched if half of that capacity is being used for simulcasting in the first decade of the next century.

Despite the intense activity in the ATV transition by broadcasters, the first services on the air with HDTV signals may be from DBS providers. Their transmission systems are already all-digital, and the conversion to HDTV was considered when the systems were designed. The DSS (digital satellite system) converter box was designed for the addition of a circuit board that would permit HDTV reception. Since many of these services provide feature films to their customers, it would seem likely that they would be among the first transmitters of ATV programming. While newer direct broadcast satellites have expanded power and channel capacity, the ATV transition may tax the ability to add new channels. It seems certain, however, that this will continue to be a dynamic and rapidly-growing segment of the broadcast industry.

While American telephone companies have slowed the pace of their entry in the television-service marketplace, they are making multibillion dollar investments in fiber optic infrastructure development. The RBOCs are merging into giant mega-companies that rival their old parent, AT&T, in size. Perhaps due to the loss of their monopoly in local phone service, these companies are expanding into every aspect of the telecommunications business. With their massive fiber transmission networks in place, they will be formidable competitors to cable companies, DBS service providers, and on-line companies in an era where video content can be transmitted as easily as e-mail. The convergence of television and computing in the form of the new standard for advanced television portends the advent of the first true telecomputers that will allow users to do word processing while watching the World Series in a corner of the screen.

A consortium of American companies is developing a new Intercast standard for embedding supplemental data in the vertical blanking interval of a television signal fed into a personal computer (Intercast, 1997). The PC viewer will be able to watch a regular over-the-air broadcast of a program such as *Nova*, while also viewing supplemental information about the program on the same screen. For instance, video of the eruption of Mount St. Helens could be viewed quarter-screen, along with downloadable maps of the mountain and additional text about volcanoes.

The merger of computing and television will expand the capabilities of systems such as Intercasting by linking the remarkable content variety of the Internet with the high production values of broadcast television. The one thing that is certain about the future of television broadcasting is that the number of channels will continue to expand, as will programming options for all viewers.

Bibliography

Ashworth, S. (1997, January 9). MCI receives DBS slot. *TV Technology*, 14.

Brinkley, J. (1996, December 25). FCC clears new standard for digital TV. *New York Times*, C1, C15.

Brown, D. (1996). A statistical update of selected American communications media. In A. E. Grant (Ed.). *Communication technology update* (5th ed.). Boston: Focal Press.

Cauley, L. (1996, December 6). Bell Atlantic, NYNEX, PacTel to close Tele-TV. *Wall Street Journal*, A2, A6.

Colman, P. (1996, July). Wireless gets digital go-ahead. *Broadcasting & Cable*, 46.

Cookson, C. (1995). Introduction of widescreen to television series production. *Symposium record of the 19th international television symposium and technical exhibition*. Montreux, Switzerland: The Symposium, 369-373.

Dickson, G. (1997, January 27). Bye-bye birdie. *Broadcasting & Cable*, 65, 66.

Dupagne, M., & Seel, P. B. (1997). *High-definition television: A global perspective*. Ames, IA: Iowa State University Press.

Federal Communications Commission. (1996). Advanced television systems and their impact upon the existing television broadcast service. *Sixth Further Notice of Proposed Rule Making*, 11 FCC Rcd. 10968.

Freed, K. (1997, January 9). S-A changes cable modem strategy. *TV Technology*, 30.

Intercast. (1997). *We interrupt your normal program to bring you something truly amazing...Intel Intercast technology*. [On-line]. Available: http://www.intercast.org.

Jessell, H. A. (1996a, February 5). The growing world of satellite TV. *Broadcasting & Cable*, 59.

Jessell, H. A. (1996b, April 8). HDTV advances in Washington: MSTV/EIA to build HDTV station. *Broadcasting & Cable*, 10.

Katz, M. (1997, January 27). Loral, Echostar getting fixed. *Broadcasting & Cable*, 68.

Martin, D. R. (1996). Wireless cable (MMDS). In A. E. Grant (Ed.). *Communication technology update* (5th ed.). Boston: Focal Press.

McConnell, C. (1996, August 19). FCC enumerates TV's future. *Broadcasting & Cable*, 17.

McConnell, C. (1997, February 3). Compromise reached on V-U digital rift. *Broadcasting & Cable*, 15.

McConville, J. (1996, December 30). Dish prices fall again. *Broadcasting & Cable*, 30.

Pavlik, J. V. (1996). *New media technology*. Boston: Allyn and Bacon.

Stow, R. L. (1993). Market penetration of HDTV. In S. M. Weiss & R. L. Stow, *NAB 1993 Guide to HDTV implementation costs* (Appendix II). Washington, DC: National Association of Broadcasters.

Tele-Communications, Inc. (1996). *HITS, headend in the sky*. Press release.

Van Tassel, J. (1997, January 27). Multicasting promoted to improve Webcasts. *Broadcasting & Cable*, 64.

Venditto, G. (1996, November). Instant video. *Internet World*, 85-95.

V

Conclusion

15

The Future of Broadcasting

August E. Grant

The technological changes detailed in the preceding chapters suggest that broadcast media around the world are approaching a major crossroads. Organizational factors, as well as technological ones, are now causing—or will soon cause—changes which promise to revolutionize virtually every area of the broadcast industry. In turn, broadcasters project that these internal changes will lead to changes in external factors, including audience behavior, the pattern of regulation, and economic support for the media.

This chapter examines the coming internal changes in the broadcast industry and projects the manner in which these changes are likely to result in broader changes in economics and audience behavior. As illustrated throughout this text, the changes themselves are profound, but the effects of these changes upon the audience and the way business is conducted will be mitigated by external factors. The end result will be new ways of producing and distributing content, but the changes for the users of the medium—the viewers and listeners—may be limited.

Four Trends in the Broadcast Media

The most important trends sweeping through broadcast media can be divided into two categories: technological and organizational. The two *technological* trends are an increase in the number of channels of programming available to viewers and a move to digital technology in all areas of television production and transmission. The two *organizational* trends are consolidation of the television and radio industries and integration of broadcasting with other media and electronic industries. This section reviews these trends, and the following section explores the impacts of these trends upon the industry, the audience, and society in general.

Perhaps the most ubiquitous trend in the global television industry is the increase in the number of channels of programming available to the audience. This increase is due to a combination of factors, with the most important of these being the introduction of new distribution technologies including cable television and direct broadcast satellite (DBS) services. Neither technology can be considered a "new" technology; cable television has existed in the United States since 1949, and DBS service began with the delivery of television signals to "backyard" satellite dishes almost as soon as the first television signals were distributed by satellites in the 1970s.

The difference is the degree to which these technologies and others are being embraced by entrepreneurs and policy makers eager to exploit the capabilities of the medium. The most difficult choice any broadcaster has to make is which type of program to deliver at a specific time when more than one type of program is available. The increase in the number of distribution channels, combined with the fact that digital compression can increase the number of channels offered by a service by a factor of four to eight, will allow many broadcasters to avoid the "either/or" decision and allow them to deliver "both."

One important enabling factor behind the increase in demand for distribution channels is a massive increase in the amount of available programming. A great deal of programming, including most entertainment programming, retains its value to viewers through multiple airings over many years, offering broadcasters an array of choices that increase every time a new program is produced. Furthermore, television programmers around the world have consistently looked to other countries for programming that can be acquired at a fraction of the cost of producing original programming. Again, every week that passes provides new options for television programmers.

The second major trend is the transition from analog to digital technology in the process of producing television programs. As discussed in Chapter 2, until recently, virtually all equipment used in television production created, stored, or manipulated continually-varying analog waveforms. These analog waveforms were subject to electronic interference, and no reproduction (whether from a video recording or a broadcast) was a perfect copy of the original waveform.

The digital revolution began with the introduction of computers which converted analog signals into digital ones, allowing manipulation of the picture using mathematical algorithms. These "digital video effects" devices were extremely expensive, but they had the capability of creating a range of video effects not possible using analog technology. The next step was the introduction of digital videotape recorders which allowed perfect reproduction of images through 100 or more "generations" (copies of copies).

Today, there is a digital version of nearly every piece of equipment used in the production of television programs. As explored in this text, the next generation of video recording equipment will abandon videotape altogether in favor of a different type of magnetic storage: fixed disk drives, similar (or the same as) those used for computer storage.

In essence, the move to digital technology has introduced computers to virtually all areas of television production. Nearly every piece of digital television equipment has as its heart a computer which controls and manipulates the digital data according to pre-programmed parameters.

One of the primary lessons from the preceding 14 chapters is the number of benefits that digital technology offers over analog technology, including quality of signal reproduction and flexibility of signal manipulation. But the most important benefit for this discussion is the manner in which it has affected the cost of high-quality television equipment.

One of the most frequently-cited trends in computer technology is "Moore's Law," the idea that, every 18 months, computer speed and memory doubles while cost is cut in half. The effect on television production equipment has been staggering. When first introduced a decade ago, digital video recorders were more expensive than the most expensive analog video recorders. As time has passed, the cost of the computer components used in video recording has dropped dramatically, while the power of these computers has increased exponentially.

The result is that an average business computer with a few modifications (including video input/output boards) can today offer most of the same functions of video recording and editing as the most advanced professional video equipment on the market—at a fraction of the cost. The quality is a step below that of professional equipment, but the next generation of computers should have no such limitation.

The end result of the digitization of television production equipment will be a dramatic reduction in the cost of high-quality video production equipment. Virtually anyone with a creative vision will be able to create and produce their own video programs at a fraction of what it formerly cost to do television production. Thus, the digitization of television offers the potential to complement the increase in distribution outlets with a corresponding increase in content available for distribution.

The digital revolution in television production is just beginning. Existing production companies are expected to move slowly toward digital technology because of the sunk investment they have in analog technology. New competitors, however, will be able to move very quickly—and very inexpensively—into these new technologies, offering the potential for a tremendous increase in the amount of available programming.

An important side effect of the introduction of digital technology leads to the first organizational trend: the integration of broadcasting with other media and electronic industries. On the technological front, computer manufacturers are beginning to provide equipment used in the television production process. Through this process, the microelectronics industry should become an important partner to the television industry, but the process will require a great deal of education in new ways of doing business for both industries.

At the same time, media companies are seen as desirable targets for merger, acquisition, and strategic partnership by other media companies, telecommunications companies, and companies involved in the computer and electronic industries. These alliances are propelled by a drive for horizontal and vertical integration as these industries become increasingly interdependent.

The second organizational trend is a direct response to the fact that other industries have set their sights on broadcasting: The radio and television industries are experiencing an unparalleled era of mergers and buyouts as broadcasters position themselves to compete in the new media landscape. This consolidation has also been driven by deregulation of ownership limitations, which is a direct response to the desire by policymakers to create a more competitive media marketplace.

Taken together, these four trends suggest that:

(1)   The number of media outlets is increasing (and will continue to increase).

(2)   The increase is fed by cheaper television production costs, economies of scale in consolidation of the television industry, and the entry of new companies, most notably computer and other microelectronics companies, into the television industry.

The extrapolation of these four trends, however, into a picture of media revolution must be tempered by analysis of factors that will not change—regardless of the degree of technological or organizational change within the media.

Patterns of Viewer Behavior

The most significant fact about the above discussion is the manner in which it ignores the viewer. In order to get an accurate picture of how the four trends discussed above will affect the television industry around the world, it is necessary to examine the role of the viewer in the process.

In almost all forms of television, especially commercial television, the viewer is the central concern of the programmer. The goal may be to entertain, inform, persuade, or even deceive, but, in all cases, the production and distribution process cannot be considered without attention to the people for whom the programming is being produced and distributed.

The most basic principle to realize in understanding viewer behavior is the fact that individual viewers watch programming in specific patterns. These patterns are governed by:

- The preferences of the viewer.

- The availability of specific programs or program types.

- The availability of the viewer to watch television.

- The preferences of other members of the viewing group (Webster & Wakshlag, 1983).

Perhaps more important for understanding and predicting the behavior of the television audience is the fact that the best predictor of what an individual will watch in the future is what that individual has watched in the past (Goodhardt, Ehrenberg, & Collins, 1987; Barwise, Ehrenberg, & Goodhardt, 1982). This phenomenon can be described as a form of "viewer inertia." In effect, it means that, regardless of the new options offered, viewers will be disproportionately likely to watch the programming they have become accustomed to watching. Indeed, one of the least explored areas of viewer behavior is habit (Rosenstein & Grant, 1997). The expectation of the strength of viewer inertia is based upon research on attitudes and behaviors in which prior behavior was found to be a better predictor of future behavior than attitude (Fishbein & Ajzen, 1975).

It is significant to note that only one of these viewer behavior factors—the availability of specific programs or program types—is affected by the four trends discussed in the first half of this chapter. There is no doubt that the changes in the television system will result in a greater variety of programming. The provision of new channels of programming will expand the number of choices available to viewers at any given point in time, and it will increase the overall number of program types available to viewers.

The key question is the manner in which *changes* in program availability affect viewer behavior. DeFleur and Ball-Rokeach (1989) suggest that viewers develop dependency relationships with television *over time*. The implication of this relationship is that any change in viewer behavior related to new channels of programming will not be instantaneous; rather, it will take place over weeks or months—even years.

Furthermore, new channels of distribution have to fight for attention in an increasingly competitive media marketplace. Neuman and de Sola Pool (1986) demonstrated that the number of media messages targeted at audience members is increasing exponentially, and the average attention to each message is undergoing a corresponding decrease. But the attention is not proportionally distributed among all available media—incumbent media share a disproportionate percentage of the audience, leaving new media (in the aggregate) sharing a disproportionately small percentage of the audience.

It is also instructive to note that the interaction between program availability and viewer preference results in a set of specific patterns of audience behavior. In examining U.S. television audiences, I have identified seven "audiences" within the larger television audience, each consuming a specific pattern of television programming (Grant, 1989; Grant, 1995). The manner in which these patterns are created across audience members suggests a significant role for interpersonal communication in determining an individual's pattern of viewing.

A related factor is the nature of television as a cultural force. In this role, television (and other mass media) provide a reflection of the culture of the viewing public. Although television can also be viewed as a force that defines culture, the potential of the medium to serve this role is limited by the acceptance of the role by viewers.

The most important corollary to television's role in the culture is the manner in which discussions of television programming have become an important part of interpersonal communication within a culture. Viewers not only adopt style and idiom through consuming television, they also talk about what they've seen. These discussions have a direct effect upon the viewing behavior of most audience members in that a person is much more likely to view a program they have discussed with their friends or co-workers, regardless of whether they have ever viewed the program before.

The end result of these two factors (the roles in culture and in interpersonal communication) is that, in any television system, viewer attention is going to be unequally distributed among available channels of programming, with a disproportionately large number of viewers watching a disproportionately small number of options. An increase in the number of channels of programming available will have a disproportionately small impact on the most popular channels and a disproportionately large impact on the least popular channels (Grant, 1994; 1993).

Another factor which must be considered is the comparative role of technology and creativity in the production process. There is little doubt that the digital production revolution will lower production costs on the technical side. It can be argued, however, that the creative side of television production will be little affected by the digital revolution. In almost every production environment, the rarest commodities are the creative roles of writing, performing, and directing. The history of television consistently demonstrates that a program with good writing, acting, etc. and average production values will consistently attract a larger audience than a poorly written, acted, or directed program with the highest production values.

Discussion

The four trends discussed in the first half of this chapter suggest a revolution in the structure and operation of the television industry. These factors will affect virtually all areas of program production and distribution, and should have a major impact on media structure.

On the other hand, the preceding discussion of viewer behavior suggests that changes in viewer behavior will be more evolutionary than revolutionary. Where new television outlets provide additional choice, some viewers will change their viewing habits to include new programming, but the expected magnitude of change is inversely related to the number of existing media. Anyone starting a new channel or program service today will have a difficult time in attracting audience away from the existing repertoire of channels.

The fact that viewer behavior may not be strongly affected by the changes in the television industry does not suggest that these changes are unimportant. The combination of lower production costs, increased channels of distribution, and privatization of media should create enormous opportunities for entrepreneurs eager to create and/or distribute television programming. The end result should be steady growth and profitability for the television industry, with a significant increase in the quantity of programs produced and in the number of jobs available in the television business.

Implications for Broadcast Education

A key issue for the future of the broadcast industry is the type of preparation that universities and other institutions must provide for the next generation of broadcasters. There will be a temptation for universities and other educational institutions to take advantage of the lower cost of digital production equipment to attempt to "catch up" with their professional brethren, allowing students to produce a product that is the technical equivalent of that produced by professional broadcasters.

There is no question that all students should become familiar with the emerging areas of non-linear editing, digital audio production, and digital graphics. On the other hand, educators must be careful not to place disproportionate emphasis on the acquisition of technical skills, especially training on a specific system that can't be translated to other systems. Emphasis on technical skills might be a mistake, especially if the goal of attaining technical quality is achieved by reducing emphasis on the creative side of the production process.

It will be much more important for universities to emphasize the roles of writing, directing, and producing. These creative skills are the rarest commodity in any broadcast production system. The best way to prepare for the increase in distribution channels is to make sure that students have essential skills in narrative and dramatic writing for broadcast. The technology used to produce television programming has evolved from live TV to film to videotape, and now to digital technology. There is certainly a new technology just around the corner that will render tomorrow's cutting-edge digital technology obsolete. Although we must prepare the next generation of broadcasters to deal with the changes in technology they will continually encounter, it is more important to train them in the basic communication skills used to create television programming.

On another front, the rapid pace of change has important implications for both future and current broadcasters. The education and training provided at the beginning of a person's career will never be enough to last a lifetime. Instead, the industry must develop a culture of lifelong learning, in which educational institutions and companies work together to ensure the provision of continuing education.

Any such continuing education process will pay important dividends to people whose jobs may be displaced as a byproduct of changing technology. As some jobs disappear (studio camera operator, for example), others will emerge (digital graphic designer, non-linear editing assistant, etc.). Close cooperation between broadcasters and educators will help ensure that educational opportunities are available that will preserve the knowledge and experience of workers who will need retaining in the future. Every occupational position in broadcasting in the next century will need to have a continuing education component to keep broadcast professionals up to speed with technological evolution on a scale that we can barely foresee at present. There is a great future for occupational complexity in the coming era of broadcasting.

Bibliography

Barwise, T. P., Ehrenberg, A. S. C., & Goodhardt, G. J. (1982). Glued to the box? Patterns of TV repeat viewing. *Journal of Communication, 32* (4), 22-29.

DeFleur, M. L., & Ball-Rokeach, S. J. (1989). *Theories of mass communication.* New York: Longman.

Fishbein, M., & Ajzen, I. (1975). *Belief, attitude, intention, and behavior: An introduction to theory and research.* Reading, MA: Addison-Wesley.

Goodhardt, G. J., Ehrenberg, A. S. C., & Collins, M. A. (1987). *The television audience: Patterns of viewing.* Brookfield, VT: Gower.

Grant, A. E. (1995, April). *Defining patterns of viewing*. Paper presented to the annual convention of the National Association of Broadcasters, Las Vegas, Nevada.

Grant, A. E. (1993, October). The 500-channel myth. *Technology South*, 5.

Grant, A. E. (1994). The impending failure of alternate delivery systems. *New Telecom Quarterly*, 2 (3), 22-28.

Grant, A. E. (1989, April). *Seven audiences: An exploration of television viewing behavior*. Paper presented to the annual convention of the Broadcast Education Association, Las Vegas, Nevada.

Neuman, W. R., & de Sola Pool, I. (1986). The flow of communications into the home. In S. J. Ball-Rokeach & M. G. Cantor (Eds.). *Media, audience, and social structure*. Beverly Hills: Sage.

Rogers, E. M. (1986). *Communication technology: The new media in society*. New York: Free Press.

Rosenstein, A., & Grant, A. E. (1997). Reconceptualizing the role of habit: A new model of television audience activity. *Journal of Broadcasting & Electronic Media*, in press.

Waterman, D. (1992). "Narrowcasting" and "broadcasting" on nonbroadcast media: A program choice model. *Communication Research*, 19 (1), 3-28.

Webster, J., & Wakshlag, J. (1983). A theory of television program choice. *Communication Research, 10* (4), 430-446.

About the Authors

Chapter 1—Introduction and Chapter 15—The Future of Broadcasting

August E. Grant formerly taught in the Department of Radio-Television-Film at the University of Texas at Austin, and has been appointed Associate Professor and Director of Research in the College of Journalism and Mass Communication at the University of South Carolina. He is editor of the annual *Communication Technology Update* (now in its fifth edition) and author of numerous research articles on new communications technologies and media audience behavior. Before he became an academic, Grant worked for eight years in local radio and television production, and he continues to act as a consultant to various broadcast organizations. His teaching experience includes a variety of basic and advanced broadcast production and communication technology courses. His recent broadcast credits include producing and directing four episodes of "Smart Show," a weekly, educational children's television program (1992-1993) and occasional radio air shifts as a talk show host.

Chapter 2—The Analog-to-Digital Transition
Chapter 14—Television Transmission

Peter B. Seel is an Assistant Professor in the Department of Journalism and Technical Communication at Colorado State University. Pete was a producer/director of television programs for 16 years prior to earning a Ph.D. in mass communication from Indiana University in 1995. His doctoral dissertation was on the U.S. standardization of HDTV, and he is the co-author of *High-Definition Television: A Global Perspective* (1997). His research interests involve the diffusion of new media technologies and their societal effects, with a special interest in multicasting audio and video over the Internet.

Pete has remained active as a television producer/director and he recently completed the documentary *Cutters of Stone* for Indiana public television affiliates. He can be reached via email at: <pseel@vines.colostate.edu>.

Chapter 3—Digital Audio Formats

D. William "Will" Moss comes from a practical background in radio and audio production, having worked extensively in commercial radio in the San Francisco Bay area. His long-standing interest in audio and audio production stems from his days as a child when he produced potboiling drama on an old mono cassette deck, and from his teenage years as an amateur musician. Although he studied marine biology as an undergraduate, he focused his interest in graduate school on broadcasting, audio, and the Internet. His Master's thesis, completed in 1995, examined the Internet as a free-speech medium and as a counterpart to traditional broadcast media. Will instructed radio classes in the Broadcast & Electronic Communication Arts Department at San Francisco State University while a graduate student.

He has recently fused his disparate professional interests, working as a producer and sound effects editor for Games Online, an Internet software development studio based in Singapore. In his dwindling spare time, Will enjoys scuba diving, photography on land and underwater, and maintaining his web presence at <http://www.mmmutants.com/>.

Chapter 4—Digital Audio Workstations

Nancy L. "Sami" Reist is Associate Professor of Broadcast and Electronic Communication Arts at San Francisco State University. She received a B.S. and an M.A. from Humboldt State University, and her Ph.D. is from the University of Minnesota. Dr. Reist's dissertation was on the effects of intercultural communication on broadcasters. At San Francisco State, she teaches courses on radio and multimedia production, media performance, intercultural communication, environmental communication, and electronic media theory and research.

She has been an active radio producer since 1975 and has produced environmentally-focused news stories for Bay Area public radio stations and for National Public Radio. Dr. Reist recently created *Sounds of Science*, a multimedia Web page that explores issues in science, culture, and ecology (see <http://beca.sfsu.edu/sos/sofshp.html>). She can be reached at: <sami@sfsu.edu>.

Chapter 5—Audio Mixers, Processors, and Microphones
Chapter 8—Video Servers (with Steve Jackson)

Jeffrey S. Wilkinson is an Assistant Professor of Broadcasting at the University of Tennessee, Knoxville. He received a B.S. in broadcasting from the University of Florida and completed an M.A. in journalism and a Ph.D. in mass communication at the University of Georgia. He held several positions in radio and television from 1979 to 1985, including news director, talk show host, anchor, general assignment reporter, beat reporter, production director, and announcer. Since the mid-1980s, Dr. Wilkinson has been involved in various research activities including private research on advertising copytesting and cable franchise price configurations. He has presented papers at several conferences and co-authored research appearing in *Journalism Quarterly* and *Journal of Mass Media Ethics*, and he recently co-authored a chapter in *Broadcast/Cable Programming* (5th ed.). His interests are radio programming, production, and management; broadcast news processes and effects; sensationalism and ethics; new technologies; and college radio. His e-mail address is: <Jeff-Wilkinson@utk.edu>.

Steve Jackson has more than 10 years of professional video experience. He directed his first nationally-broadcast television program for the Home Shopping Network in 1986 at age 17, and eventually directed over 3,000 hours of live programming for them. Steve previously worked as a technician for the engineering department at KCCI TV-8 in Des Moines, Iowa. He directed the program *Ebony Visions* for Vision Cable in Clearwater Florida, and has done freelance work as a director, lighting grip, technical director, and videographer on numerous sport programs, variety shows, and commercials. Steve holds a B.S. from Franklin Pierce College and currently is an M.A. candidate at the University of Tennessee where he assists with seminars in non-linear editing for the College of Communication's Department of Broadcasting. He is also a producer/technician for the University of Tennessee's Telemedia Services department, and is a consultant on visual theory and product display. His e-mail address is: <goathead@utk.edu>.

Chapter 6—Cameras and Lenses
Chapter 13—Radio Transmission

David Sedman is an Assistant Professor in the Television-Radio Department at Southern Methodist University in Dallas, Texas. He began his career in local radio in the mid-1980s. He returned to school and completed his Ph.D. at Bowling Green State University in 1990. Since that time, David has taught and been involved in a variety of video projects, ranging from corporate videos to satellite-fed tele-courses.

Dr. Sedman's main research interest is new communication technologies. He has used this interest to create Web pages, produce interactive CD-ROMs, and write articles and book chapters devoted to new technology. He labels himself an "early adopter" who buys many useful and trivial gadgets. David welcomes questions about new technology including digital cameras, new innovations in radio, or any consumer electronic devices. He can be reached at <dsedman@mail.smu.edu>.

Chapter 7—Videotape Formats

James C. Foust is an Assistant Professor in the Department of Journalism at Bowling Green State University. He has worked as a news videographer and editor and currently advises BG-24, a student-run television newscast at the university. His research interests are new technology and electronic media history. He has written chapters on desktop video and computer technology for *Communication Technology Update* and a chapter on interactive media for *Television Production: Disciplines and Techniques*. He has also published in scholarly journals. He can be reached by e-mail at <jfoust@bgnet.bgsu.edu>.

Chapter 9—Linear Editing Systems

Sheila E. Schroeder is a Ph.D. candidate in the Department of Telecommunications at Indiana University. Beside five years of corporate video management experience, Sheila has recently moved into documentary production. She served as co-videographer on her latest project, *Sisters of the Earth*, produced for the PBS affiliate in Bloomington, Indiana. Sheila also volunteers at WTIU as the pre-game and post-game host for IU women's basketball. This activity reflects her primary research concern: women, sports, and media. Sheila's dissertation, *Hoop Meanings: A Feminist Cultural Analysis of Women's Professional Basketball in the United States*, examines the role of the media in the two new women's basketball leagues. She is especially interested in grass-roots publications and the use of the Internet in the social construction of the professional female basketball player.

Chapter 10—Non-Linear Editing Systems

Ron Osgood is Director of Undergraduate Programs and Facilities for the Department of Telecommunications at Indiana University. He teaches courses in the design and production area and recently developed a course in digital video production. Before coming to Indiana University in 1987, Ron held several positions as producer and manager in the video production field. He is an active member of the International Television Association where he was a member of the national board of directors and chairperson of the conference program planning committee. Ron is currently studying the use of porfolio/demo reels in the job search process.

Chapter 11—Video Production Switchers, Special Effects Generators, and Digital Video Effects

Suzanne H. Williams, Associate Professor, has been on the faculty of Trinity University since 1987. Prior to returning to graduate school, she was a broadcast engineer at WITI-TV in Milwaukee, Wisconsin, and during graduate school co-produced and directed videotapes which received both regional and national distribution. Dr. Williams has taught television production for over 15 years and is a co-founder of the closed-circuit television channel at Trinity. As chair of the production division of the Broadcast Education Association (BEA), she co-founded the division's Juried Faculty Production Competition, and she currently serves on the BEA board of directors. The major areas of concern for her teaching and research have been the understanding and production of television messages, children's television programming, and animation. Her writing on television production includes co-authoring a recent book chapter on the assessment of production education and numerous articles and presentations on teaching production and interpreting television messages. She is also currently on the executive council and is the newsletter editor for the Society for Animation Studies and has written articles and presented numerous papers on the values found in children's television and animation. She can be reached at <swilliam@trinity.edu>.

Chapter 12—Lighting Technology

Bill Holshevnikoff has been lighting and shooting award-winning broadcast, corporate and documentary programming for over 15 years. He received his formal education from the Telecommunications and Film Department at San Diego State University. Since that time, he has worked for clients such as Ritz-Carlton Hotels, the BBC, Mercedes Benz, PepsiCo, SEGA, Infinity, Sun Microsystems, and created studio lighting designs for news, interview, and game show sets in the United States and Eastern Europe.

Considered a leader in lighting education, Bill's commitment to research and development in lighting keeps him on the leading edge of lighting techniques for video and film production. His experience as an educator includes the production of over a dozen highly-successful lighting education videos, including his own *Power of Lighting* video series, and over 100 featured columns in popular trade publications, such as *American Cinematographer* and *Video Systems*. Since 1992, Bill has completed three 30-city lecture tours on lighting techniques that have been seen by thousands of industry professionals across the United States and Canada.

Glossary

ADSL (Asymmetrical Digital Subscriber Line). A system of compression and transmission that allows broadband signals up to 6 Mb/s to be carried over twisted pair copper wire for relatively short distances.

Advanced television (ATV). Television technologies that offer improvement in existing television systems.

Algorithm. A specific formula used to modify a signal. For example, the key to a digital compression system is the algorithm that eliminates redundancy.

AM (amplitude modulation). A method of superimposing a signal on a carrier wave in which the strength (or amplitude) of the carrier wave is continuously varied. AM radio and the video portion of an NTSC television signal use amplitude modulation.

Analog. A continuously varying signal or wave. As with all waves, analog waves are susceptible to interference which can change the character of the wave.

ANSI (American National Standards Institute). An official body within the United States delegated with the responsibility for defining standards.

ASCII (American Standard Code for Information Interchange). Assigns specific letters, numbers, and control codes to the 256 different combinations of zeroes and ones in a byte.

Aspect ratio. In visual media, the ratio of the screen width to height. Ordinary television has an aspect ratio of 4:3, while high-definition television is "wider" with an aspect ratio of 16:9 (or 5.33:3).

Asynchronous. Occurring at different times. For example, electronic mail is asynchronous communication because it does not require the sender and receiver to be connected at the same time.

ATSC (Advanced Television Systems Committee). A committee created by the FCC to oversee the process of developing advanced television standards in the United States.

ATV (advanced television). The generic term used to describe any television system that represents an improvement over the NTSC standard. SDTV and HDTV are two examples of ATV.

ATM (Asynchronous Transfer Mode). A method of data transportation whereby fixed-length packets are sent over a switched network. Speeds of up to over two gigabits per second can be achieved, making it suitable for carrying voice, video, and data.

B

Backward compatibility. A characteristic of a new technology that allows materials created using the previous technology to be played or manipulated on the new technology. For example, S-VHS video equipment is backward compatible with VHS, allowing any VHS tape to be played on any S-VHS machine.

Bandwidth. A measure of capacity of communications media. Greater bandwidth allows communication of more information in a given period of time.

Basic rate ISDN (BRI-ISDN). The basic rate ISDN interface provides two 64 Kb/s channels (called B channels) to carry voice or data and one 16 Kb/s signaling channel (the D channel) for call information.

Bit. A single unit of data, either a one or a zero, used in digital data communications. When discussing digital data, a small "b" refers to bits and a capital "B" refers to bytes.

Broadband. An adjective used to describe large-capacity networks that are able to carry several services at the same time, such as data, voice, and video.

Byte. A compilation of bits, seven bits in accordance with ASCII standards and eight bits in accordance with EBCDIC standards.

C

C-band. Low-frequency (1 GHz to 10 GHz) microwave communication. Used for both terrestrial and satellite communications. C-band satellites use relatively low power and require relatively large receiving dishes.

Cart. An enclosed tape cartridge.

Cart machine. A tape player designed to hold and play carts. Simple cart machines hold a single cart; others may hold 100 carts or more.

CCD (charge coupled device). A solid-state camera pickup device that converts an optical image into an electrical signal.

CCITT (International Telegraph and Telephone Consultative Committee). CCITT is the former name of the international regulatory body that defines international telecommunications and data communications standards. It has been renamed the Telecommunications Standards Sector of the International Telecommunications Union.

CD-ROM (Compact Disc-Read Only Memory). The use of compact discs to store text, data, and other digitized information instead of—or in addition to—audio. One CD-ROM can store up to 700 megabytes of data.

CD-R. A recordable CD-ROM.

Central processing unit (CPU). The "brains" of a computer, which uses a stored program to manipulate information.

Coaxial cable. A type of "pipe" for electronic signals. An inner conductor is surrounded by a neutral material, which is then covered by a metal "shield" that prevents the signal from escaping the cable.

Codec (COmpression/DECompression). A device used to compress and decompress digital video signals.

COFDM (Coded Orthogonal Frequency Division Multiplexing). A flexible protocol for the transmission of advanced television signals that allows simultaneous transmission of multiple signals at the same time.

Color temperature. A measure of the color of light. The lower the color temperature, the redder the light; higher color temperatures describe bluer light. The term is derived from the concept that all objects give off light when heated, with the color of light changing as the temperature of the object changes.

Component video. A video signal in which the luminance (Y) and color (C) information are distributed via two separate channels.

Composite video. A video signal in which the color information (C) is hidden inside the luminance signal (Y), allowing the video to be distributed in a single channel.

Compression. The process of reducing the amount of information necessary to transmit a specific audio, video, or data signal.

D

Decompression. The process of restoring a specific video, audio, or data signal from a compressed signal. Decompressed signals take up considerably more bandwidth than compressed signals.

Digital. See Digital signal.

Digital audio broadcasting (DAB). Radio broadcasting that uses digital signals instead of analog to provide improved sound quality.

Digital audio radio service (DARS). See Digital audio broadcasting.

Digital audiotape (DAT). An audio recording format that stores digital information on 4mm tape.

Digital audio workstation (DAW). A computer designed to record, edit, process, and manipulate audio signals converted to digital form.

Digital commercial systems. A computer system configured to record and play back commercials for a radio or television station. The audio signals for the computer are stored on a hard drive, along with traffic information identifying when specific commercials should be played.

Digital signal. A signal that takes on only two values, off or on, typically represented by "0" or "1." Digital signals require less power but (typically) more bandwidth than analog, and copies of digital signals are *exactly* like the original.

Digital video compression. The process of eliminating redundancy or reducing the level of detail in a video signal in order to reduce the amount of information which must be transmitted or stored.

Digital versatile disk (DVD). A silvery digital disk similar to a CD that can store up to 20 times the data, audio, or video available on a single CD or CD-ROM.

Digitizing. The process of converting an analog signal to a digital one and storing it in digital form.

Direct broadcast satellites (DBS). High-powered satellites designed to beam television signals directly to viewers with special receiving equipment.

Downlink. Any antenna designed to receive a signal from a communication satellite.

E

EDL (edit decision list). In video editing, a sequential list of all of the video and audio pieces which must be assembled to create a program. Also refers to a computer-generated library of numerical information that instructs an edit controller to operate videotape recorders to assemble a program.

Electromagnetic spectrum. The set of electromagnetic frequencies that includes radio waves, microwave, infrared, visible light, ultraviolet rays, and gamma rays. Communication is possible through the electromagnetic spectrum by radiation and reception of radio waves at a specific frequency.

ENG (electronic news gathering). The process of using portable video cameras, audio equipment, etc. in the process of reporting the news.

F

Federal Communications Commission (FCC). The U.S. federal government organization responsible for the regulation of broadcasting, cable, telephony, satellites, and other communications media.

Fiber optics. Thin strands of ultrapure glass or plastic which can be used to carry light waves from one location to another.

Field. One scan of an interlaced television picture consisting of all of the odd or all of the even lines. Two fields (one odd and one even) are needed for a frame, which is a single complete video picture.

FireWire. A digital connector from a video camera to a personal computer's hard drive that eliminates the need for a video capture card in the computer.

FM (frequency modulation). A method of superimposing a signal on a carrier wave in which the frequency on the carrier wave is continuously varied. FM radio and the audio portion of an NTSC television signal use frequency modulation.

Footprint. The coverage area of a satellite signal, which can be focused to cover specific geographical areas.

Frame. One complete picture in a video signal or motion picture film. The persistence of vision of the human eye allows a series of frames to be projected in sequence to create the illusion of a moving image.

Full-motion video. The projection of 20 or more frames (or still images) per second to give the eye the perception of movement. Broadcast video in the United States uses 30 frames per second, and most film technologies use 24 frames per second.

G

Gateway. A specialized node on a computer network that provides a connection between that network and other networks. Gateways are critical to the architecture of WANs and the Internet.

Geosynchronous orbit. A satellite orbit directly above the equator at 22,300 miles. At that distance, a satellite orbits at a speed that matches the revolution of the earth so that, from the earth, the satellite appears to remain in a fixed position.

Gigabyte. 1,000,000,000 bytes, or 1,000 megabytes (see Byte).

Graphical user interface (GUI). A computer operating system that is based upon icons and visual relationships rather than text. Windows and the Macintosh computer use GUIs because they are more user friendly.

H

Hard disk drive. A disk made of material similar to videotape backed by a rigid circular platter. The disk spins rapidly, and is written and read by an arm that carries the read/write heads. Because of the speed at which the disk is spinning, the arm can find data on the platter very rapidly.

High-definition television (HDTV). Any television system that provides a significant improvement in existing television systems. Most HDTV systems offer more than 1,000 scan lines, in a wider aspect ratio, with superior color and sound fidelity.

I

Image stabilizer. A feature in camcorders that lessens the shakiness of the picture either optically or digitally.

Interactive TV. A television system in which the user interacts with the program in such a manner that the program sequence will change for each user.

Intercasting. The process of using the Internet to transmit audio and/or video programming to a mass audience.

Interlaced scanning. The process of displaying an image using two scans of a screen, with the first providing all the even numbered lines and the second providing the odd-numbered lines.

Intranet. A local or wide area computer network that serves a single entity such as a corporation or school. Intranets can have all of the features of the Internet, including electronic mail, file transfer, and hypertext links. The primary difference between the two is that an Intranet has set boundaries while the Internet has no such boundaries.

ISDN (Integrated Services Digital Network). A planned hierarchy of digital switching and transmission systems synchronized to transmit all signals in digital form, offering greatly increased capacity over analog networks.

ISO (International Organization of Standardization). Develops, coordinates, and promulgates international standards that facilitate world trade.

ITU (International Telecommunications Union). A U.N. organization that coordinates use of the spectrum and creation of technical standards for communication equipment.

J

JPEG (Joint Photographic Experts Group). A unit of the ISO. Also refers to the digital compression standard for still images created by this group.

K

Kilobyte. 1,000 bytes (see Byte).

Ku-band. A set of microwave frequencies (12 GHz to 14 GHz) used exclusively for satellite communication. Compared with C-band, the higher frequencies produce shorter waves and require smaller receiving dishes.

L

Laser. From the acronym for Light Amplification by Stimulated Emission of Radiation. A laser usually consists of a light-amplifying medium placed between two mirrors. Light not perfectly aligned with the mirrors escapes out the sides, but light perfectly aligned will be amplified. One mirror is made partially transparent. The result is an amplified beam of light that emerges through the partially transparent mirror.

Linear editing. The process of assembling a program in pieces starting from the beginning of the program and proceeding in order to the end. With linear editing, it is difficult to go back to an earlier point to add material or re-edit unless the segment to be replaced or re-edited is exactly the same length as the segment it is replacing.

Local area network (LAN). A network connecting a number of computers to each other or to a central server so that the computers can share programs and files.

Local exchange carrier (LEC). A local telephone company.

Lossless. A type of video compression that does not discard information, and allows the original signal to be recovered in the decompression process.

Lossy. A type of video compression that disposes of (usually imperceptible) parts of a video signal, so that the original signal can never be precisely recreated in the decompression process. Lossy compression usually requires less bandwidth than lossless compression.

M

Mb/s. Megabits per second.

Megabyte. 1,000,000 bytes, or 1,000 kilobytes (see Byte).

MIPS (millions of instructions per second). This is a common measure of the speed of a computer processor.

MMDS (Multichannel, Multipoint Distribution Systems). A service similar to cable television that uses microwaves to distribute the signals instead of coaxial cable. MMDS is therefore better suited to sparsely-populated areas than cable.

Modem (MOdulator/DEModulator). Enables transmission of a digital signal, such as that generated by a computer, over an analog network, such as the telephone network.

Monochromatic. Light or other radiation with one single frequency or wavelength. Since no light is perfectly monochromatic, the term is used loosely to describe any light of a single color over a very narrow band of wavelengths.

Motion JPEG. A video compression algorithm developed by the Joint Photographic Experts Group that reduces the amount of data needed to transmit a video image by reducing the amount of data needed to represent each individual picture.

MPEG (Moving Pictures Experts Group). A committee formed by the ISO to set standards for digital compression of full-motion video. Also stands for the digital compression standard created by the committee that produces VHS-quality video.

MPEG-1. An international standard for the digital compression of VHS-quality, full-motion video.

MPEG-2. An international standard for the digital compression of broadcast-quality, full-motion video.

Multimedia. The combination of video, audio, and text in a single platform or presentation.

Multiplexing. Transmitting several messages or signals simultaneously over the same circuit or frequency.

Must-carry. A set of rules requiring cable operators to carry all local broadcast television stations.

N

Nanometer. One billionth of a meter. Did you know that "nano" comes from the Greek word for dwarf?

Nodes. Routers or switches on a broadband network that provide a possible link from point A to point B across a network.

Noise. Unwanted information added to a signal in the process of transmission, reception, or amplification.

Non-linear editing. The process of putting together a program by assembling pieces in any order. In non-linear editing, additions, deletions, or changes can be made at any point without affecting edits prior or subsequent to that point.

NTSC (National Television System Committee). The group responsible for setting the U.S. standard for color television in the 1950s.

O

Octet. A byte; more specifically, an eight-bit byte. The origins of the octet trace back to when different networks had different byte sizes. Octet was coined to identify the eight-bit byte size.

Off-line editing. A preliminary editing process designed to create a "rough cut" and edit decision list that will be used to construct the final, "on-line" edit.

On-line editing. The final editing phase where all original elements and effects are edited and mixed to create a program ready for distribution.

P

Perceptual encoding. A method of digital compression that reduces the amount of information in an audio or video signal by eliminating parts of the signal that cannot be perceived by an audience member.

Peripheral. An external device that increases the capabilities of a communication system.

Pixel. The smallest element of a computer display. The more pixels in a display, the greater the resolution.

Pixelization. An artifact of digital video production or compression techniques in which detail is lost. Unwanted pixelization results in loss of detail in both lines and color, and often makes angled lines seem rough or jagged. A pixelization effect can also be deliberately created to reduce or eliminate detail.

Point-to-multipoint service. A communication technology designed for broadcast communications, where one sender simultaneously sends a message to an unlimited number of receivers.

Point-to-point service. A communication technology designed for closed-circuit communications between two points such as a telephone circuit.

Post-production. In television production, the process of mixing, editing, or adding graphics to a program after the initial video and audio have been recorded.

Primary-rate ISDN (PRI-ISDN). The primary rate ISDN interface provides twenty-three 64 Kb/s channels (called B channels) to carry voice or data and one 16 Kb/s signaling channel (the D channel) for call information.

Printing to tape. The process of recording the output from a digital video system or computer on analog format for broadcast or distribution.

Progressive scanning. A video display system that scans all the lines in a video display sequentially.

Prosumer. A term used to describe mid-range video equipment that provides higher quality, reliability, and/or price than consumer equipment, but lower quality, reliability, and price than typical professional equipment.

Q

QuickTime. A computer video playback system that enables a computer to automatically adjust video frame rates and image resolution so that sound and motion are synchronized during playback.

R

RAID (Redundant Array of Inexpensive Disks). A set of large, interconnected, inexpensive, fast hard disk drives designed to store and play video. Some RAID drives are configured to access data very quickly, and others are designed to act as a redundant backup system, assuring that data is not lost in case of drive failure.

Random access. The ability to retrieve any portion of a stored signal on demand without having to sequentially review the entire signal.

RBDS (radio broadcast data services). A service that uses a stream of digital data encoded within a radio broadcast to provide a stream of information to specially-configured receivers.

RDS (radio data services). See RBDS.

Rendering. The final stage in a digital production process where all elements are blended together to create the final product.

Retransmission consent. The right of a television station to prohibit retransmission of its signal by a cable company. Under the 1992 Cable Act, U.S. television stations may choose between must-carry and retransmission consent.

RF (radio frequency). Electromagnetic carrier waves upon which audio, video, or data signals can be superimposed for transmission.

Router. The central switching device in a computer network that directs and controls the flow of data through the network.

S

Sampling. In digitizing an analog signal, the process of measuring the analog wave at discrete points in time. The number of times a wave is sampled is known as the "sampling rate."

Sampling rate. The number of times a wave is sampled in the process of digitizing a signal. The greater the sampling rate (the more times the wave is measured during a given time period), the more accurately the digital signal will represent the original analog signal. Most sampling rates are based on Nyquist's theorem, which states that a sampling rate must be at least twice the highest frequency being measured.

SCSI (small computer system interface). [Pronounced "scuzzy."] A type of interface between computers and peripherals that allows faster communication than most other interface standards.

SDTV (standard definition television). A digital television broadcast signal that contains approximately the same level of detail as an analog NTSC television signal, but which may be transmitted in a fraction of the bandwidth. One television channel can therefore be used to transmit a number of SDTV signals simultaneously.

Simulcasting. The process of transmitting the same programming on two or more broadcast stations at the same time.

SMPTE. Society of Motion Picture and Television Engineers.

SONET (Synchronous Optical Network). A set of protocols and standards for transmission of data over fiber optic networks that allows simultaneous transmission of circuit- and packet-switched data over the same network. SONET networks are capable of extremely high-speed data transmission (as of 1996, up to three gigabytes per second), and it is compatible with a variety of network protocols including ATM, FDDI, and broadband ISDN.

Spot beam. A satellite signal targeted at a small area or footprint. By concentrating the signal in a smaller area, the signal strength increases in the reception area.

Switcher. A device that allows a user to select or blend a variety of video sources, including live video, recorded video, and graphics, into a single video output.

Sync or *synchronization.* The part of a television signal that contains information identifying the beginning of individual fields and lines. Using a common sync source for all video equipment in a television station ensures that each piece of equipment starts a new line, field, or frame at the same time, allowing interconnection and switching among multiple pieces of television production equipment without artifacts.

Synchronous transmission. The transmission of data at a fixed rate, based on a master clock, between the transmitter and receiver.

T

TCP/IP (transmission control protocol/Internet protocol). The set of standards developed for the Internet that enables almost any computer network to send and receive messages from and through other networks. The "transmission control protocol" refers to a process of dividing the data in a message into packets that are numbered and placed in virtual envelopes. "Internet protocol" then furnishes a second "envelope" in which the first is placed by providing a standardized set of conventions necessary for routing data packets. In sum, the IP part of a data packet contains the routing information, and the TCP determines how many packets are necessary for a message or file, along with providing error correction information.

Terabyte. 1,000,000,000,000 bytes, or 1,000 gigabytes (see Byte).

Time code. Information added to an audio or video signal that provides each picture with a unique number identifying the hour, minute, second, frame number, and reel number for that individual picture.

Transponder. The part of a satellite that receives an incoming signal from an uplink and retransmits it on a different frequency to a downlink.

TVRO (television receive only). A satellite dish used to receive television signals from a satellite.

Twisted pair. The set of two copper wires used to connect a telephone customer with a switching office. The bandwidth of twisted pair is extremely small compared with coaxial cable or fiber optics.

U

UHF (ultra-high frequency). Television channels numbered from 14 through 83.

Universal service. In telecommunications policy, the principle that an interactive telecommunications service must be available to everyone within a community in order to increase the utility and value of the network for all users.

Uplink. An antenna that transmits a signal to a satellite for relay back to earth.

V

Vertical blanking interval. The first 21 lines of a video signal that are not displayed on a television set. Lines one through nine are used to synchronize the television signal, but lines 10 through 21 are available for the transmission of a variety of data services including color information, teletext, utility services, and graphics.

Vertical integration. The ownership of more than one function of production or distribution by a single company, so that the company, in effect, becomes its own customer.

VHF (very high frequency). Television channels numbered from two through 13.

Video on demand (VOD). A video delivery system which allows a user to select a movie or other program from a library of dozens, hundreds, or even thousands of options. VOD allows the user to start, stop, fast-forward, pause, and review the program during playback.

Video server. A powerful computer configured to store and transmit video images in digital form. Video servers can serve as a form of video switching and storage, allowing transmission of many different video images simultanously through different network paths.

W

Wide area network (WAN). A network that interconnects geographically-distributed computers or LANs.

Wireless cable. See MMDS.

WORM (Write once, read many). A recording format that allows a single recording pass on a medium, but which may be played back repeatedly.

X

X.25 data protocol. A packet switching standard developed in the mid-1970s for transmission of data over twisted pair copper wire.

Index